Don't Water the Stick:
The Path of the Psyche

Don't Water the Stick

The path of the psyche

BERNARD WILLEMSEN
WITH PENNY MARGOLIS

QUASAR BOOKS
WINNIPEG, CANADA

Canadian Cataloguing in Publication Data

Willemsen, Bernard, 1936—
    Don't Water the Stick: the path of the psyche

1st ed.
Includes Index.
ISBN 0-9680351-0-8

    1. Parapsychology.   2. Mind and body.   3. Mental
healing.   I. Margolis, Penny, 1945—   II. Title.

BF161.W54 1996   133.8   C96-900133-9

Editing: Alison Mitchell
Cover design: Adrian van Noort
Printed and bound in Canada by Kromar Printing Ltd.

This edition is printed on acid-free paper.

For my daughters Pamela and Tricia,
who give me the great joy of being their dad

Contents

Acknowledgments

First, to my mentor and dear friend Robert F. Downing, with whom I began my journey over 20 years ago and who, by booting me out of his psychic development circle, taught me my first lesson about spirituality—those who think they know it all have the most to learn. Of all the lessons I have since learned and am still learning, his is the most precious to me.

To Dr. Joan Townsend, whose anthropological research in psychic and spiritual activities in North America provided me with the opportunity to demonstrate and put to the test my clairvoyant capabilities in relation to human energy and healing. Over the two years or more that we worked together, I came to value her intellectual honesty, scholarship, great dedication to her subject and, above all, her friendship. I am deeply grateful for her interest in my work and in my development, and for the validation I received from her.

To Dr. Richard Fogel, friend and chiropractor extraordinaire, for his humility and generosity of spirit. Over the nine years that we have worked together, Rick has freely offered both his time and energy, helping me to understand what I was seeing, and providing me with the opportunity to hone my skill of diagnostic imagery.

To my friend Farrell Fleming, Executive Director of Creative Retirement Manitoba, for inviting me
to teach in his program where I could freely share my
knowledge.

To Brian Head, Principal of Continuing Edu-
cation in St. James-Assiniboia, for recognizing the
value of what I wanted to share.

To Brenda ('Brendie') Malek Koffler, for her
support, friendship and commitment to my psychic
development, particularly during the research period.

To all the students who participated in the
personal development groups over the past ten years,
giving me the opportunity and joy of sharing the
teachings and the honour of guiding them in their
learning.

To all the others who have touched my life in a
variety of ways, helping me to grow and fulfill my
purpose.

Finally, to my devoted and loving wife Penny,
from whom I have learned, among many other things,
that seeing is not necessarily believing, and who hung
in with me, humbly accepting the role of scribe,
notwithstanding her reluctance to acknowledge the
psyche and its reality. Besides the lessons I have
learned through sleeping with the 'devil's advocate,'
I have found her to be my best critic, due to her intellectual thoroughness, together with her support of and
belief in my work and my truth. For her persistence in

helping me to capture in words the knowledge I have to share, she has my deepest gratitude.

Foreword

I was very pleased to be asked to write the foreword for this book. I have known Bernard Willemsen (whom I call Ben) for ten years as a friend, as the teacher of a series of classes I coordinated for seniors, and as an adviser with whom I have consulted occasionally on my own personal health issues.

As Executive Director of a seniors' educational program, I have watched Ben work with older people in a variety of courses. For many years his classes were among our most popular. It might seem odd that older people would be attracted to programs in psychic development. But this is unusual only if one holds the late 20th century North American view of retirement and old age as a time of recreation, at best, or decline and illness, at worst. In many cultures, both present and past, old age is seen as the time to fully engage the spiritual development process. This is intensely personal work, often undertaken with the help of one or more teachers. The 'work' of old age is work on oneself. In Winnipeg, some of those seniors with an interest in this work chose to study with Ben. After they had exhausted the course offerings of our organization, they went on to Ben's private classes. Many of them remain students of his to this day.

His basic view of the spiritual is something that I, along with many others, have come to share over the years. Whatever the spiritual ultimately is, it must be rooted in everyday life, in our relationship with nature. Even if it involves extraordinary experiences in the mountains, it must ultimately be tested in our ordinary lives and in our intimate relationships with family and friends.

The basic premise of Ben's work is that there is energy associated with the human body, that this energy has a particular structure, and that it is a part of a universal energy system. Although many still doubt this premise, it is becoming more difficult to deny. Indeed, if Einstein was correct in equating matter and energy ($e=mc^2$), there must be a human energy system.

For thousands of years, human beings have explored the psyche, using abilities which appear to be latent in all of us, but which only come to full fruition in a few, such as the shamans throughout the ages. The maps they have drawn of the psychic landscape bear a remarkable similarity to each other. I have no doubt that, as new technologies give rise to machines that can map the energy systems associated with the human body, the vision they provide will coincide with that of ancient and modern seers. The next great advance in medicine will be in 'energy medicine.'

It is often said that we use only a small portion of our brains. What would a human being who used significantly more be like? One possible answer is that he would be animating far more of his psychic abilities than most do at present. Compared with the length of existence of other species, we are in the earliest stages of human evolution. One can surmise that we have much evolving to do before we are fully able to use all of our latent capabilities. Ben and others like him give us a glimpse of what some of those capabilities might be.

For readers of this book, it is important to understand that Ben is speaking from his experience, not his belief structure. The book represents what he has seen and what he knows, not what he has imagined or what he believes. As he says in his Introduction, this book represents his truth. He does not say *the* truth, but rather *his* truth. The book itself is an invitation to the reader to discover his or her own truth. It is not that this truth is uninformed by reflection. The process of writing this book and his work with his students and clients over the years have brought increasingly sophisticated levels of reflection to his experience. The core concepts and realizations, however, come directly from his experience and represent his knowledge.

Throughout it all, Ben has remained a profoundly *human* being. There are no false airs or pretensions. He has resisted the temptation to become a 'guru' or spiritual leader. He has entered fully and with great energy into the dance of ordinary life. Recently, as he nears sixty years of age, he has begun to explore his early childhood under the guidance of a therapist. To hear him describe his work (and play) in this area is to understand the intensity with which he lives and the joy (even amidst the pain and sorrow) that he brings to life.

The process of writing this book has involved an intense collaboration between Ben and his wife Penny. They have my admiration, both for the result, and for the process itself. Not many marriages could withstand the nature of this joint work. In their case, it seems to have definitely strengthened the relationship. I am looking forward to their continuing collaboration and the succeeding volumes in what I trust will become a significant body of work in the realm of the psyche.

Farrell Fleming, Ph.D.(Cand.)

Preface

When I was a boy, my mother always told the story about how a stork was on its way to the palace with a baby boy. As he flew over our house, he noticed that the kitchen window was open. He was very tired, having come from a great distance, so he flew in the open window and deposited me inside. As a small child, I spent a great deal of time wondering how that big stork managed to get through our small kitchen window. My mother had said it happened, so it must have happened.

Perhaps it was because of this story that, during my childhood, I spent a great deal of time learning to fly. My first attempts were made up and down the stairs of our apartment building in Rotterdam. I was about five or six at the time. I would get into bed, pull the covers over my head, and feel myself going down into darkness. Moments later I emerged from the darkness and found myself in the hallway outside my room, leaving my body behind in the bed. It seemed like such a simple trick.

Once in the hallway, I started going up and down the stairs, and to my surprise and delight, found that I could float above them. In the beginning, I floated from wall to wall, bumping into things, not knowing how to stop myself. After a while, I learned how to control my movements by focusing on exactly where I wanted to end up.

One night, with some apprehension, I dove head first down the stairs, directing myself with my eyes. I flew down all three flights of stairs and was able to control my flight without incident. This game was fun and I played it frequently, going faster and faster down the staircase each time.

After I had mastered flying down the staircase, I ventured outside our house. Around the corner was the Schie channel where I often played. I went to the channel, wondering whether I could fly over the water. Because I couldn't swim, I worried about what would happen if I got tired half-way across. So I practised flying beside the channel and, in a brave moment, flew out across the water for a few yards before hightailing it back. It took many visits to the channel before I got up the courage to fly all the way across.

After moving to Amsterdam, I continued my nightly forays. The biggest problem I had was navigating around streetcar wires. For some reason, I couldn't manage to fly above them, and I was frightened to fly beneath them for fear of colliding with a streetcar or truck. One night, on one of my trips, I noticed someone climbing the wall of a four-storey apartment building. I realized then that I might be able to fly higher by moving up in stages, so this was what I learned to do.

To get to the top of a building, I would fly to the highest point I could reach, usually a window ledge on the second floor. I would rest there for a while and then try to fly to a higher point. It usually took me three stages to reach the top of our apartment building. Once on the roof, I would walk around, enjoying the enormous flat expanse overlooking our neighbourhood. Sometimes I would see someone else on the roof. Soon I learned to fly from building to building until I reached the roof of the church. From there, by stages, I flew to the church steeple. By then I was usually exhausted, and would rest on a ledge of the bell tower. I never went inside the tower, always fearing its darkness. After I'd rested, I would fly home again, rooftop to rooftop, resting a few more times along the way. I must have told my mother about my trips, because one day she told me to stay away from the psyche, warning me that it was dangerous. By then I was thirteen.

At the age of 21, after settling in Canada, I began asking myself questions: Why was I here? What was the purpose of earth? What kept nature in balance? How did the insects come to be? Was someone responsible? Was there a God? Why were children born with handicaps? How could the Germans, during the war, have read the same bible as us?

With all these questions running through my mind, I once again began experimenting with my psyche, attempting to get free of my body as I did when I was a child. I read some books about the Tibetan lamas and Zen, and others about psychics and clairvoyants. I'd never been a good reader, even in my native language, but these books seemed so familiar to me that I was able to read them without difficulty. One day, something in my head told me that I'd read enough. After that, I lost interest in reading.

There were nights that I would lie awake with a question on my mind about life and, somehow, by morning, I would have an answer. I didn't know where the answers came from, but I knew they didn't come from my own head. This happened often during my work in the engineering field, beginning when I was nearly 30. The company I was working for would have a problem that needed solving, or an idea that needed to be developed. These were problems with which they had sometimes struggled for years, unable to reach a solution. Although I didn't have the knowledge to even begin thinking about many of these problems, I would still wonder whether I might be able to solve them. I'd get a sick feeling in the pit of my stomach and, before I knew it, I had offered to do it. Later, I would be panic-stricken and wonder what could have possessed me to even consider taking on such a task. Late at night, something would start working in my head, as though pieces of a puzzle were falling together, and I would suddenly 'get' a solution. It seemed to come out of nowhere, and I would rush to put it down on paper. By then, it was usually far into the night. To my great delight, my solutions were always successful.

Because of these and other experiences, I realized that someone or something out there had the knowledge I was looking for and could answer my questions. Sometimes, in my frustration about not knowing, I would pull my car over to the side of the road, run into the middle of a field, look up at the sky and curse God or whoever was up there.

One day, when I was living in Orillia, I went to visit a psychic reader, just for fun. As soon as I sat down beside her she said, "You are very psychic." I was flabbergasted, not understanding what she meant. She said I should meet an acquaintance of hers who led a spiritual circle, and she offered to telephone him on my behalf.

Shortly afterwards, I became a member of Robert's circle. Over the course of that year, many psychic capabilities unfolded within me, including psychometry, clairvoyance and precognition. In addition to these, I started practising distance healing and relaying messages from spirit. Instead of feeling good about what was happening, however, I was becoming more and more confused. I was looking for answers, but now I had even more questions.

One day, I was standing at the living room window of our farmhouse, looking out at the two magnificent blue spruce trees in our front yard. Although the trees were on my property, I never took them for granted; I always looked at them anew. I didn't feel that they belonged to me. As I stood there thinking about what had happened to me over the past year—how my sense of reality was being turned inside out—I began asking, "Why me?"

Without warning, I felt a hard bang on my head. It was like an explosion. Then I saw my body with a beam of golden light coming from the top of my head and going straight upwards. Before I had time to react, I was moving at a tremendous speed. I could see nothing but stars all around me. Down between my feet, I saw the earth, half the size of a basketball, brightly lit. I cannot describe the feeling I had, moving at such a speed amidst a sea of stars. When I looked down again, the earth had shrunk to the size of a golf ball and, a moment later, it vanished from sight. I kept travelling at that same phenomenal speed for some time.

Suddenly, all movement ceased, as though someone had put on the brakes. I was suspended in time and space, motionless, and everything was still. I looked around, awestruck by the countless stars surrounding me, yet I felt completely aware and without fear.

My attention was drawn to something above my right shoulder. I looked up and saw a bright orange sphere. It appeared to be close by, yet it was far beyond my reach. While observing it, I experienced a sensation unlike anything I had ever felt before. The word that comes closest to describing it is *ecstasy*. That moment is permanently etched in my being.

Then, abruptly, I was in motion again and the next thing I knew, I re-entered my body with a tremendous jolt. There I stood in my living-room, disoriented and unable to associate with my surroundings. A strange feeling came over me and I heard a voice telling me to look in a mirror. I walked to the bathroom and, steadying myself against the vanity, I lifted my eyes up to the mirror. I began to panic; I didn't recognize the face in the mirror. The voice spoke again, louder this time, saying, "Look at the eyes." I looked, but still there was no recognition. The panic mounted and I began to look away. Again I heard, "Keep on looking at the eyes!" This time I persisted and gradually started to realize that I was in those eyes.

The sense of unreality and unfamiliarity stayed with me for three seemingly endless days. Then, I had an argument with my wife that startled me back into a more normal frame of mind. It was then that I began to wonder if I had gone crazy. I telephoned my mentor Robert, telling him about my strange journey and my fears for my sanity. He suggested I stay where I was while he called someone whom he thought might help me make sense of my experience.

Later that day, I met with Robert and his friend David, a priest who taught at a theological college nearby. After listening to me recount the story or my journey, and the experiences that led up to it, he reassured me that I wasn't insane; in fact, he had read about other people throughout history who had

had similar experiences. Then, he began to ask me questions. Many of them were related to events and concepts about which I had no conscious knowledge. Yet I answered him without hesitation.

Over the following few days, it gradually dawned on me that, after 20 years of asking "Why?", I no longer had any questions. It seemed as though, in less than a moment, I'd received an entire library of knowledge and, in that same moment, it had become an integral part of me. There was no room for debate; this was what I *knew.*

To this day, I still don't know everything there is in the library. I may never be able to understand it all. As questions are raised, however, and as I continue with my learning, more and more of the knowledge comes forward.

The six years following my extraordinary journey were difficult ones. I continued doing psychic work—healing, advising and communicating with spirits—but I remained confused and without clear direction. Then, for a period of time, I walked away from all my involvements with the psyche, trying to re-establish a sense of normality in my life. But things went from bad to worse. I lost my position as a design engineer when the manufacturing company was sold, my marriage began to collapse and, by the end of that six-year period, I found myself in Winnipeg, single, broke, and emotionally devastated.

Within an incredibly short period of time, however, the pieces of my life's puzzle began falling into place. People appeared in my life unexpectedly as though directed to help me by some unseen intelligence. I entered a three-year period of intensive psychic and spiritual development, involving long periods of meditative exercises during which I was directed and guided by spirit teachers.* I went through many stages in my psychic development, coming to understand more fully how the psyche works and becoming more deeply acquainted with the power of its energy. I experienced tremendous pain as my third eye was opened. I was then taught how to activate and use it, both to see and to send energy over a distance. For several years during this period, I also participated in a research study on psychic and spiritual healing.

Overnight, everything turned inside out again. All of a sudden, I found myself struggling to recover from an emergency operation following a burst appendix, having somehow managed to drive myself to the hospital while hallucinating. The six months of my rehabilitation brought unprecedented challenge to my fragile ego system, resulting in my gaining some important self-awareness. Since that time, I have continued to work at closing the gap between my psychic

---

* I will share more deeply about this period of my development in my forthcoming book, *Beyond a Shadow: The path of spiritual evolution.*

and spiritual knowledge on the one hand, and my level of personal awareness on the other. In the process, I have been attempting to share my knowledge, through teaching and counselling, and now, through this book.

Introduction

We inhabit a physical world. Just as a fish cannot see beyond the water in which it lives, we cannot see beyond our material boundaries. But the physical dimension is only a small part of our reality.

Most of us have had an experience that could not be explained in terms of physical laws. Usually, it's forgotten or tucked away somewhere in our memories. Because there is an unwillingness within our society to recognize and identify these experiences, we eventually stop having them, or else we keep them to ourselves. As we get older, however, we may return to them and once again wonder what they mean. Often, however, there is no one with whom we can share our thoughts and no one to answer our questions.

Our hunger to know, which comes from the psyche, is neither acknowledged nor recognized for what it is. The answers we get, if any, are patronizing and, ultimately, controlling. They are designed to shut us up, giving us nothing to work with—no basis from which to explore. Because our need to find meaning is not validated, we are discouraged from seeking our own knowledge. Think of the five-year-old asking where he came from and receiving the reply, "You are a gift from God." Or the 13-year-old who asks what will happen when he dies, and is told, "You'll go to heaven, of course." Or even the 18-year-old who wants to talk about the meaning of life and is dismissed with "Don't worry about it, just get married and have some kids, and you'll find out soon enough."

At various times in Western history, people who walked the path of the psyche were tortured and put to death. It was and still is believed that an individual who departs from the accepted truths of his time, particularly one who stands outside of institutionalized religion, becomes a threat to the social order. This is because he is not dependent upon it and, therefore, cannot be controlled by it. Throughout history, however, there have been healers whose methods were based on the psyche and for whom the psyche was an integral part of life. These healers have helped to hold their societies together by providing a link between physical and psychic reality. Far from threatening the social order, they brought stability to their people.

When we choose to ignore the psyche, we neglect a major part of ourselves. In the process, we lose our individuality, our creativity, and our relationship with the divine aspect of life—our *knowing*—however we may experience it. Also, when we are unaware of the psyche, we have a tendency to misuse or waste our energy.

Many people are never taught to take responsibility for themselves. Instead, they put themselves in the hands of doctors, preachers, gurus, teachers, and even God. Once we are led to believe that we will be taken care of, it becomes very difficult to give up that sense of protection (however illusory it may be) so that we may pursue our own truths. Our religions forbid us to seek answers outside their own dogmatic teachings, creating immense fear and reinforcing our need for the protection and reassurance they provide. The medical community, too, discourages us from looking beyond its carefully controlled boundaries for alternative ways of healing.

How are we then to take back responsibility for our own lives? Isn't it easier, after all, to let someone else take the blame for the unfortunate things that happen to us? When we ignore the psyche, however, we deny ourselves the opportunity to discover the meaning and purpose of our lives.

Then there is the issue of money and power. Money has become the most important value in our society. It dictates what we desire, what is available to us, and what we 'need.' It controls our thoughts. If psychic abilities could be manufactured, bottled and patented, the psyche would never be suppressed or ignored; on the contrary, it would become a gigantic industry. The prevailing reality is no more or less than that which keeps someone's pockets well lined.

Interest in the psyche has grown tremendously over the past 20 years, however. More and more people are growing up, becoming angry, and beginning to challenge beliefs that were previously unquestioned. Perhaps this is because the earth is going through a major evolutionary step, and we are in a panic as we perceive our physical world to be falling apart. We are now desperate to find a purpose for it all. This is similar to the urge we feel, as we age and our bodies begin to fail us, to become seekers and search for the meaning of life. Through awareness of the psyche, we can embark upon a journey towards our own truth and our place within the universe. In this way we can become *knowers* instead of believers.

About ten years ago, I began to share a small part of my knowledge of the psyche in a course which I called 'Applied psychics,' offered through a seniors organization. A second course, called 'The spirit and I,' would follow a year later. These courses went through numerous transformations over the years, while at the same time, others were added, including 'The art of transmitting healing energy,' 'The psyche and personal development,' 'Exploring the meaning of God,' and 'Spirituality, living and growing.' These courses are now beginning to take the form of a series of books on the subject of 'human energy dynamics.' This one, focusing on awareness of the psyche, is the first.

In the second volume, *Beyond a Shadow,* I will focus on the interrelationship between the physical and spiritual worlds and show how our physical life is only a first step in the human cycle.

This book represents my truth—that which I unshakably *know*. It is my hope that it will not only help to validate the experiences of others, but also enable them to take a step forward in their awareness of the psyche and, ultimately, their total self.

Note: Throughout the book, I have referred to actual cases for the purpose of illustrating certain themes. In order to protect the privacy of my clients, I have altered some of the information about them.

CHAPTER 1

The Psyche and its Body

When was the last time you stood in front of a mirror and asked yourself, Why do I have a nose? Why do I have eyes? Why do I have ears? Chances are, you haven't done it recently, because these are things we normally take for granted. But we can not hope to understand the psyche without an awareness of the importance and the purpose of our physical self, which is, in a manner of speaking, the psyche's vehicle. Without the body, the psyche could not exist, just as oxygen could not exist without the tree.

A human consists of two major components, as does every living thing: a physical body and an energy being or psyche. Their combined purpose is to create mind.[*]

The physical body consists, first, of a head, which houses a brain as well as all the other tools for our survival: eyes to find food, see danger and communicate; a nose to smell what is good and what is bad; and so on. In this way, we are like most other animals.

The brain has to be kept alive, and this is one of the functions of the body. It is basically a fuel cell, converting food into energy. It has two legs to move it from point A to point B, and two arms with which it defends and feeds itself, as well as caring for young. The other function of the body is to reproduce.

Let's take a closer look at the psyche. The Latin word *psyche*, from the Greek word for 'breath,' originally referred to the soul or spirit that animates physical life. The word has since been used to refer, variously, to the mind, the higher self and the soul, among other things. We will use the word *psyche* to mean all the energies and forces associated with either the soul or the physical body.

In all living things on earth, we find a drive to grow. In humans, it is the soul—the essence of our being—which provides us with that drive. When the soul takes possession of a baby, it forms an energy body or auric field which surrounds the

---

[*] See p. 9

infant. This energy field is the main part of the
psyche. In the human adult, the energy field takes
the shape of an egg, nine feet high and seven feet
wide. The energy egg consists of many different layers, with the physical body standing in the middle of
it. One of these layers, called the flowing aura, is the
bridge between the psyche and the body and it is
necessary for our survival. It flows upwards through
the body and back down around it. (The flowing
aura is the subject of Chapter three.) The energy egg
with all its layers, combined with the energies of the
physical body, make up a distinctive pattern, unique
to each person and, together, make up the total
psyche or energy being.

There are two aspects of the psyche being,
corresponding to the two types of energy of which it
is composed: the physical/sexual, relating to the
body, and the intellectual/spiritual, relating to the
soul. The physical/sexual aspect, which we will call
the *body psyche*, includes all the energies responsible
for life. One of these is the body intelligence, found
both within the brain and along the spine. The body
intelligence is responsible for the operation, mainte-
nance and survival of the physical body. Another of
the physical/sexual energies is found in the energy
envelopes that surround and nourish each organ in
the body. In addition, there is the energy responsible
for procreation or the drive for physical life. Known
as 'Kundalini,' it rests at the base of the body near
the reproductive system and, according to yogic

philosophy, it is the cosmic energy in bodies. (In certain yogic practices, an attempt is made to raise this energy to the crown of the head in order to reach a state of spiritual enlightenment.) While the physical body merges with the earth after death, these physical/sexual energies will merge with the universe.

The intellectual/spiritual aspect of the psyche is made up of all the energies of the soul and its drive, including the layers of the energy egg, and the mind. We will call this aspect the *psyche self.* When the body dies, these energies remain for a period of time as a spirit and eventually merge with the universe.[*]

All of these energies, whether associated with the body or the soul, are imperceptible to our physical senses. Each vibrates at a different rate or frequency and each has a distinct place and purpose; they do not intermix.

The mind is composed of four major parts. The first three are mind energies produced by the brain. Of these three, the first consists of data or information stored in and around the brain, and the second, of information stored along the spine. The third part consists of live memories—emotionally charged memories that have not been dealt with or resolved—stored elsewhere in the body. We will

---

[*] See Willemsen: *Beyond a Shadow: The Path of Spiritual Evolution,* forthcoming (1997)

explore this part of the mind more fully in chapter three.

The fourth component of mind is the ego system, which is the identity or sense of self. The ego system determines how we perceive ourselves, and affects the way in which we interpret things. It is formed over the first 18 years of our lives, through interaction with our parents or caregivers, teachers and peers. The raw material out of which the ego is shaped is the soul drive. Some people may have difficulty with this notion, since ego is often viewed as a negative force and soul as a positive one. But let's look more deeply into this.

Once the soul takes possession of a baby, it starts to drive the infant in the same way that a tree is driven to grow or a plant to blossom. Just as a tree will do everything to survive, without thought or emotion, so will a human being through his soul drive. It is for this reason that we say the soul and its drive are totally selfish.

In humans and higher animals, however, that soul drive, or will to live, is not enough by itself to guarantee survival. We need to be nurtured and taught. As we are taught to survive, we are also being taught who we are. The soul drive is the clay out of which our identities are moulded or shaped by our parents and caregivers, and later by our teachers and peers.

We now see that, just as the brain produces energies which become mind, the soul provides energies out of which the ego is formed. Thus, it becomes clearer that there is not a strict division between our physical bodies and our psyches. Both the soul, which brings the will to live, and the brain, which produces mind, are necessary for growth and learning.

As we saw earlier, the flowing aura is the bridge between the psyche, or more specifically the *psyche self,* and the physical body. At birth, it is driven entirely by the soul. Gradually, as our minds and ego systems develop, they begin to influence the aura's flow, and the aura eventually comes to mirror who we are, including our feelings and attitudes, both past and present. It is through the aura that the psyche communicates with the physical body. As it flows through the body, it will profoundly influence our physical health.

It is now apparent that the physical body, although primarily the vehicle for the psyche, is of no less importance than the psyche itself. Which is, after all, more important, the tree or the apple? The answer is often determined by one's perspective. For us, the apple is food, and the tree is the bearer of the food. Therefore, we place a higher value on the tree. But the tree farmer knows that without seeds there would be no trees and so, for him, the seed—that is, the apple—is more important.

We saw earlier that the combined purpose of the body and the psyche is to produce mind. If we

12

adopt a universal perspective, we will see that the creation of mind energy depends upon the continuation of physical life. Therefore, we need to see our essence in its simplest form, that is, as the carrier of the seed. Otherwise, we have no foundation upon which to grow, or to know where we are going.

Questions

What does it mean that our purpose is to create mind?

The existence of the universe depends upon the continuous growth of all its parts; without growth there is decay. The soul can be seen as a molecule of the universe with an innate drive to grow. When the soul takes possession of the baby, giving it the will to live and develop, the infant begins to take in and process sensory information. This causes the· brain to produce mind energies. Throughout our lives, as we continue to learn, the mind continues to grow. Eventually, long after the death of the body, the soul will grow by consuming that mind.* The sole purpose of life is to contribute to the growth of the soul.

---

* See Willemsen (forthcoming)

Some people might ask, "How can I, who am so tiny compared with the universe, make a contribution to its existence?" To answer that question, I will pose another: "Is a single grain of wheat important?" Our first inclination may be to answer "no." But if one grain of wheat has no value, it follows that the same is true of two grains and three grains, and so on. From this, we have to conclude that all the wheat in the world is without value. Clearly, this is not so, because without wheat there would be no life. Therefore, one grain of wheat *is* important and so, too, is the individual mind.

As a child I was told a story about a powerful king who asked a wise man for advice. Pleased with the advice, the king asked the wise man what he would like in return. In response, the man brought a chess board to the king and requested that a grain of wheat be placed on the first square of the board, and that the number of grains be doubled on the next square, and that that number be doubled on the following one, and so on, until the whole board was filled in this manner. The king laughed, thinking that his 'wise' man wasn't asking for very much. He soon discovered, however, that there was not enough grain in the land to fill the entire chess board.

If we picture ourselves within the vast scope of the universe, we may come to the conclusion that we are, as the Zen masters say, "but a thought." But it is precisely because of that thought that life exists in the universe.

Do all living things have souls?

The essence of the soul is knowledge and its purpose is growth. In order to grow, it requires mind, which must be furnished by a living being. But only those beings that have brains and, consequently, can learn, are able to produce mind. Without a brain, there can be no soul. Thus, while all living things have a drive to grow, not all have—or, more precisely, *are driven by*—souls.

Trees have a drive to grow. While the tree itself does not have a soul, its purpose is to support the growth of soul in other living beings. It does this by providing oxygen to our bodies, thus ensuring our survival. Unlike the soul, which contains knowledge from all of its previous incarnations, the energy that drives the tree is simply a universal fuel, or the 'soul of the earth,' giving life to all vegetation and simple life forms. Regardless of whether or not they have a soul, however, all living things on the earth contribute to the existence of the universe.

If the brain is damaged, what happens to mind?

Mind is part of the psyche and, as such, it can never be destroyed. The healthy brain manipulates information stored in the mind, acquires new information and, at times, brings it forward in a physical manifestation, such as speech. If the brain is

15

damaged, any one of these functions may be impaired or lost entirely, but the mind continues to exist.

What does it mean that the soul takes possession of the infant? Isn't it the infant who comes to possess a soul?

All life exists for the sake of soul growth. The soul does not belong to us; we belong to it. One could even say that the earth belongs to the soul and, as part of the earth, so too does the human body.

The infant does not *have* or *possess* a soul; the soul possesses the infant. Our belief that the soul belongs to us is a strong one, often carrying with it the false conviction that the soul's previous incarnations are actually our own past lives. Some of us even try to gain access to those lives, hoping that they may help us to better understand ourselves. Often, however, we are merely looking for a way to justify or excuse our behaviour in this life, and avoid taking responsibility for our present circumstances.

When does the soul take possession of the infant?

Many people believe that the soul enters the baby upon conception or shortly thereafter. Because the fetus is part of the mother both physically and psychically, however, no other soul can take possession of it. The fetus, inside the mother's body, belongs to the same soul and is part of its energy field. No soul will allow another soul force to take possession of its body or any part of that body. Consequently, the fetus also shares its mother's flowing aura. As it passes through the fetus, her aura supports and vitalizes the developing body and its psyche.*

Not until after birth does the soul takes possession of the infant. As we look at a pregnant woman, using our psyches, we may see a brightness in her abdomen. This is the energy envelope in which the fetus is developing and growing—not, as some might think, a distinct soul force. When the fetus kicks, this is not a sign of an identity but rather a response of the body intelligence, which is flexing its muscles, so to speak. Not until after birth, when the soul takes possession of the baby and starts to drive it, does an identity come into being. When a woman gives birth to a baby, she does not give birth to a being with a separate identity, but to a part of herself which develops an identity after a soul takes possession of it.

---

* See Chapter 3, "The Flowing Aura"

CHAPTER 2

The
Ego
System

Ego is the core of the psyche self; it is the essence of the 'I am.' As we saw earlier, the raw material of ego is the soul drive or life force. As this force is shaped, it becomes ego. The parents or care-givers are responsible for shaping the soul drive, through their interaction with the child from infancy through adolescence. Any behaviour that the parents exhibit towards their child has the effect of teaching the child and, consequently, shaping his ego. This teaching or shaping process will occur regardless of whether the parents are aware of their responsibility.

Just as important in the child's ego development is that which he is *not* taught by the parent. That which is not taught leaves a void in the ego, the 'I am not,' which later becomes a need as the ego develops. This will become clearer later in the chapter.

The soul drive is a totally selfish force. We usually view selfishness as a negative trait, but let's look at it in another way. In order to survive, a tree will send roots in any direction: up, down, around—even through sewer pipes—in its search for nourishment. Its canopy of leaves will reach in all directions to obtain sunlight. In return, the tree will give oxygen and fruit. This same drive, responsible for survival, is found within every living thing. In humans, it comes from the soul and causes us to develop an identity and to learn. In the sense that it impels us to maintain life at virtually any cost, the soul drive is a selfish force.

The soul, upon taking possession of the infant, drives according to its unique combination of inherited qualities.[*] Each person's path is based on these qualities. The *character* of the soul drive is determined by the astrological setting of the planets within our solar system at the moment that the soul takes possession of the infant. Individual character affects the way a person walks his or her path. Everything else about one's ego is determined by the

---

* See Willemsen (forthcoming)

20

shaping of the soul drive, through experience and teaching.

As we saw earlier, the shaping of the soul drive into the 'I am' or ego takes place during infancy, childhood and adolescence. It is shaped by those who nurture the physical body, specifically by the way in which they respond to the child's physical and emotional needs—whether or not they show love and acceptance, give encouragement and praise, set boundaries and use discipline.

The most important building block of the ego, and the foundation on which everything is built, is trust. This part of the ego is shaped as soon as the infant learns that, whenever he feels discomfort and cries, he will be cared for. This caring comes in the form of both physical and psychological nurturing, through feeding, holding and being talked to. As the parent responds to the infant's discomfort time and time again, the infant quickly learns to depend upon this nurturing. In other words, he learns to trust that he will be responded to and his needs will be met. Through this trust relationship, the child gets the message that he is okay.

The foundation of trust is laid in infancy, during feeding. If the baby is not held, but is instead given a bottle propped up on a pillow, the ego is *not* being shaped. A bottle held by a pillow does not breathe, talk, touch, hold, look or smile and, therefore, cannot shape the ego.

It is not simply a matter of the bottle versus the breast. Even a child who is breast-fed can lack nurturing if he is fed irregularly or handled roughly. The same is true if the mother is preoccupied with something and the baby senses her absence. Under these circumstances, there may be little difference between a propped-up bottle and a breast. A distracted mother does not shape her child's ego.

In some children, the trust aspect of the ego is shaped very quickly and easily, through feeding, handling and talking to. In other children, the soul drive may require more input before trust is established. In some cases, the child may not be content to be by herself and may need more handling and attention in order to feel comfortable. The building of trust in another child may require the use of discipline. Some children, for example, need to have clearly set boundaries in order for them to learn that they are okay. Each child has different needs; in a family with two children who are both treated the same way, one may not be getting the right ingredients to build trust.

Why are boundaries so important in the development of trust? When parents set boundaries, they take control of the child's environment, rather than allowing the child to take control of theirs. Some children feel okay only after they learn that they cannot manipulate their parents. If the parent is always attending to the child, even after all identifiable needs have been met (for example, picking up a baby who makes the slightest sound, or postponing bedtime) the child never comes to feel that he is okay. As a result, this child will crave more and more attention, never feeling satisfied with the amount he receives.

The purpose of boundaries is to guide a child; within them, he can move freely, knowing that he is secure and cared for. Without consistent boundaries, he will have a false sense of his own limitations; he will never learn to distinguish between what he can and cannot do. Such a child may feel anxious, not trusting himself with any task, or he may feel driven to find boundaries against which to test himself, at times leading to extreme behaviours. When boundaries are clearly set, the child develops trust in the directive or input from the parent, and the 'I am' comes to feel at ease.

Praise is also essential for the developing ego. To feel worthy, a child needs to know that he has pleased his parent. "Mummy, mummy, look!" is the same as the child's request for food. In both cases the child is asking for nourishment; the first, psychological and the second, physical. Without acknowledgment and compliments from the parent, the child will never see his success as an accomplishment and, as a result, his ego will not be fed.

As it is being shaped, the developing ego depends upon continuous input from the parent for its nourishment. Take the example of a one-year-old learning to climb stairs. If he continually receives encouragement and a helping hand and is always applauded for his efforts, he will gradually build up confidence in himself. As a result, the ego will be nourished, and he will learn that he is okay.

Also critical to the child's ego development is the acknowledgment and acceptance of his feelings. Just as infants cry when they feel hungry, children cry when they feel badly. It is important that they be allowed to communicate their ego pain. When this communication is allowed, the child feels at ease because he can express his need. In addition, the parent's response to that need nourishes and, therefore, shapes the ego.

Often in our society, male children are not allowed to cry when they feel badly. As a result, feelings are kept hidden, and cannot be dealt with. When a child is not allowed to express his feelings, there will be an unresolved hunger, or void, in the ego. As a result, the child will become an adult with an insecurity. Whenever he feels any emotion, he will think that he is not okay or that he is weak.

Acceptance of oneself as a sexual being is an extremely important part of the ego. It is important that the child be happy with being a boy or a girl, as the case may be, and this includes feeling good about how he or she looks. Children need compliments about their appearance, as well as acknowledgment of their sexuality, in order for the sexual part of the ego to be fed. This acknowledgment eventually develops into feeling comfortable with one's sexuality.

As the ego continues to develop in young adulthood, so too does trust, but trust takes on a different face and meaning. In a young child, trust develops by virtue of the parent-nurturer living up to the child's expectations. The child comes to trust that he will be taken care of, that his feelings will be acknowledged and accepted; in other words, that he is okay. At the same time, the child has learned not to trust that which might hurt him. Physical survival is the root of infant trust.

As the child grows up, the infant trust has to change into a state of knowledge or understanding more suitable for the adult world. A change of perspective is required for this transition to occur, and in many people, it never does. The principle of infant trust does not work in an adult world because others will not live up to our expectations as the parent-nurturer did. When an adult who still operates on the principle of infant trust says, "I trust you," this trust is unconditional and places a tremendous burden upon the person to whom he says it. From the adult perspective, unlike that of infant trust, we acknowledge that others will live up to their own expectations and fill their own needs, not ours. In this way, we allow others space to be themselves.

The following example illustrates the way in which infant trust differs from the adult state of understanding: Can you trust a crocodile? From the perspective of infant trust, the answer would be "No"; if we were to approach a crocodile and trust it as we did the parent-nurturer, it would eat us. It would do so without anger or malice; it merely eats to survive. From an adult's perspective, however, trust is not an issue. An adult neither trusts nor distrusts the crocodile. He simply expects the crocodile to behave as a crocodile. If the crocodile is hungry, it will eat whatever is available, animal or human.

Without the foundation of infant trust and the later stages of childhood trust, it is very difficult for us to develop the understanding we need to function in the adult world. A person who never trusted as an infant will never be able to feel okay with who he is. He may take consolation in judging or criticizing others, which prevents him from having to face his own feelings of inadequacy. This person will tend to avoid those people he cannot manipulate. His behaviour does not come from the ego, but from the *ego defence.*

The ego system consists of two components: the pure ego, and the ego defence. While the pure ego, or the 'I am,' is shaped out of the soul drive, the ego defence is created by the mind in an attempt to compensate for the 'I am not.' It is formed when any of the basic ingredients required by the ego is lacking. Together, the ego and the ego defence make up who we are and how we perceive ourselves.

When the infant cannot depend upon having his basic needs met—if his hunger is not always satisfied, or his cries bring an inconsistent response—then a void is left within the ego. The infant may experience a deep sense of anxiety, even a fear of dying, and basic trust will fail to develop. As a result, a pattern of behaviour is created in an attempt to overcome the pain of that void. It is like a blanket which covers the vulnerable part of the ego, in an attempt to soothe it. This blanket is the ego defence.

The ego defence begins by covering over or soothing the hurt, and ends up having to feed and sustain itself. Once its cycle of self-feeding begins, it will use any means, including denial, forgetfulness, lying, stealing, over-achieving, and manipulation of others to perpetuate itself. Its need is self-centred and insatiable.

The person who was never taught infant trust will develop an attitude or behaviour—for example, becoming guarded, wary and manipulative—in an attempt to protect and comfort himself. It is as though the ego defence is saying "I will feed you" or "I will look after you." Although he tries to fill the void in his ego system by hoarding things, or drawing attention to himself, the needs of his ego are never filled, only temporarily subdued.

Why do his efforts fail? Because we look to our parents to fill our needs, just as a dog looks to its master for strokes. We can't or won't accept nurturing from anyone else. We keep waiting—growing more and more angry—for our parents to fill those needs, sometimes even after they're elderly and senile. As a result, the voids in our ego system remain, and any nurturing we do receive merely helps to sustain the ego defence.

The pendulum can also swing to the other side, as in the case of the so-called 'perfect parents.' These are the ones who would do absolutely anything for their child. They are constantly worried that he is unhappy and, if he is unhappy, so are they. He fills an empty place within their own lives. These overprotective parents view the setting of boundaries as a cruel act rather than a liberating one. They wait on their child hand and foot, satisfying all his needs, as they perceive them to be. He is never challenged or made to do anything for himself. His efforts to gain mastery of simple tasks, like putting on clothes, tying his shoelaces or cleaning up his room, are not supported by his parents. They want to be the perfect nurturers and, as a result, he never develops self-confidence. He may feel inadequate in comparison to his peers. His trust will never develop beyond infant trust—the trust that he will be taken care of.

As an adult, he will have a tremendous handicap because he will expect everyone around him to live up to his expectations unfailingly. Such a person is not only a psychological cripple, but often incapable of looking after himself physically as well. He will depend on others to do things for him in order to feel okay. His point of view is that the world owes him something. The void in his undeveloped ego will trigger a strong ego defence to offset his feelings of helplessness and incompetence. He may manipulate those around him in an attempt to gain nurturing from them. If they fail to nurture him adequately, he will view them as incompetent or uncaring. The ego defence will do anything to protect him from feeling needy. In extreme cases, when the ego defence cannot offset the ego pain, he may escape into depression, signaling his denial of self (in other words, a denial of his needs and feelings). Suicide is the ultimate denial of self.

We mentioned earlier that compliments and praise are essential to ego development. Too often, however, parents give compliments solely on the basis of physical attractiveness, "Aren't you pretty," for example, or "What a lovely dress." Praising a child only for her physical appearance is like feeding someone a steady diet of unhealthy food: the stomach gets full but the body doesn't get the nourishment it needs for proper development. If the child receives too many compliments about her appearance, the other parts of her ego will not be fed. She will become overly focused on her appearance and, as a result, her ego will constantly be hungry for compliments. However, these compliments will never feed the ego, but will instead contribute to the ego defence. The need for compliments may become like a drug addiction.

Let's look at another situation in which the ego defence can come into play. Take the child who is constantly being compared with her older sister. "Martha can do that, why can't you?" Throughout her entire childhood, her own abilities, talents and interests are overlooked. She constantly receives the message that she is less than Martha—that she is not good enough—while Martha receives the message that she is better. Because neither one learns that she is okay by virtue of her own qualities, both are denied the nourishment their egos require. In order to compensate, the ego defence takes over and begins self-feeding. In order to feel okay, Martha will constantly try to be better than others, while her sister will always be comparing herself with others.

Another example is the teenaged boy who is not as handy as his father. Every time he wants to fix his bike or do some gardening, his dad always knows how to do it better. Whatever the son does, he constantly gets the message that he can't do it well enough. The more often this message is conveyed, the hungrier his ego becomes. He keeps waiting for his father to tell him that he is proud of him, but the compliments never come, and he continues to accept his father's behaviour towards him.

As a result, a typical ego defence behaviour begins to emerge. In order to compensate for the 'I am not,' the son will continually try to prove that he can not only do it, but do it better than anyone else. His ego defence will drive him to compete with everybody. He won't be a team player because he will be forever seeking the praise that he never received from his father. Even when he does receive praise from others, it will not feed the hungry ego, but only subdue the ego defence.

This is the nature of the ego defence: covering over the void yet not allowing anything nourishing to fill it. The result is that the ego defence gets more and more clever and manipulative, while the ego itself is never given a chance to grow. If we are always on the defensive, our self-feeding can never be more than a band-aid for ego pain. It will never fill the empty places within.

As we have seen, the ego defence develops spontaneously in response to the unfilled needs of the ego system. While the foundation for our adult identities is laid long before we reach adulthood, we still have the potential to shape our egos after we have left our formative years behind. Our growth lies in reclaiming this potential.

Questions

How can we nurture our own egos?

The first step in nurturing our own egos is to take responsibility for ourselves—both the 'I am' and the 'I am not'—and to accept ourselves uncon-ditionally. We need to stop blaming others for the voids in our ego systems; just as each of us is the unique product of all our learning and experience, so were our parents the products of theirs. We cannot be anything other than what we are now and, as such, we are just as 'normal' as everyone else.

Unless we take responsibility for ourselves, change is impossible. When we say, "I can't help behaving this way because I was neglected as a child," we are blaming others for our behaviour. Instead, we should say, "I behave the way I do because I haven't yet learned to behave differently," or "I behave this way because I choose to." Only from this perspective can the process of healing begin.

The next step in learning to nurture the ego is to become aware of how we are defending it and why. As we become more honest with ourselves, our needs will begin to surface. This may cause us to feel vulnerable and insecure. We may worry about how others will see us, wondering if they will still like or respect us when they find out how small, inadequate or frightened we feel inside. We may find that our needs date from childhood, adolescence, or even as far back as infancy, perhaps stemming from emotional difficulties or trauma we experienced during our ego development. If trust, for example, was not established in infancy, it will now take many years to build and will, in the beginning, require the help of a counsellor or therapist. As trust develops and we become aware of the needs of our ego, we will be best able to meet them through a caring personal relationship.

This process of personal development takes great courage; it is very difficult and often painful. However, it can also be an exciting journey of self-discovery.

How important is love to the developing ego?

Love is the most powerful, all-encompassing force within the universe. It is the force out of which everything else emerges. It is the root of everything that supports physical life. Like the soul drive, love is totally selfish.

The word *love* has many different meanings. A young man, seeing an attractive young woman walking by, says, "I love her," when he really means, "I desire her." A woman says to her partner, "I love you," when, in essence, she is really saying "I respect you." A man 'loves' his dog because she makes him look like the best hunter.

Love is not the exclusive domain of humans; it is found in the animal world as well. In this context, however, we tend to think of it as merely instinct. Love is the force that drives the bird to show off its plumage to attract a mate. It is the force that brings the bird back to her nest with her prey, so that she can feed her young. The same force brings the lioness back to her cubs to teach them how to hunt and survive. Love drives the bee to gather nectar, thereby pollinating the flower, and the dog to protect her master without regard for her own life.

It is because of love that a man will return to his partner with the rewards of his labour; it is also because of love that a mother will nurture, protect and teach her child, thereby shaping his ego. In this way, love is essential to the developing 'I am.'

The love force is not always 'nice.' It can move us not only to comfort, but also to kill, in order to protect life. It causes us to say "no" to our children so that they learn to accept boundaries, have respect for others, and practice self-control. This will enable them, later in life, to cope with disappointment, accept their limitations, and overcome obstacles. Love in its purest form is seen in the weaning process, as the parent prepares the child to become independent.

Our own need for love can actually prevent us from giving our children the love they require for proper ego development. A needy parent will discourage or delay the development of self-sufficiency in her child because she derives her worth from being needed. She may even convince herself that the unnatural dependence she has fostered in her child is actually love. In contrast, the loving parent prepares her offspring for life and, as soon as his wings are strong enough, she will encourage him to fly.

Contrary to what many people think, the ego can never be fed merely with the words "I love you." This is something that many of us say frequently to our children and to each other. But what are we really saying? Some of us use it to excuse our behaviour as parents: "Maybe I'm not the greatest parent, but I love you." Others say it when they really mean "You fill my needs." Sometimes we send it out as a signal, hoping to get the response "I love you, too," which is often only an echo. Or we use "I love you" as a promissory note, but fail to keep the promise.

Only by telling our children and our partners what we really mean when we say "I love you" can their ego systems be fed. "You make me feel good," "You give meaning to my life," "I like the way you treat me," "I respect your values," "You make me feel wanted," "I can be vulnerable with you," "I like being with you," "You turn me on," or "I need you to love me" all convey more meaning and sincerity than an empty "I love you."

Can our inner child ever grow up completely?

Just as it takes nine months for a baby to develop, it takes the first 18 years of life for the ego to be shaped. The ego is the foundation upon which the rest of one's life is built. No matter how old we are chronologically, nor how much experience or wisdom we acquire, our ego systems are fully formed at the age of 18. Our growth lies in developing them to their full potential.

Let's imagine that the ego system is a floor made of bricks and each brick represents one aspect of the ego. By the age of 18, one's "floor" would be laid and he could start to build his life on it. However, let's say that by the time he was 13, one aspect of his ego had still not been shaped, leaving a hole in his floor where a brick is missing. At the end of 18 years, there might be several holes in the floor where bricks are missing. At this point, he is an 18-year-old with a handicap. He tries to compensate for the missing bricks by building and maintaining a barrier around the holes to avoid falling in and getting hurt. This barrier is the ego defence.

When people talk about the 'inner child,' it is as though there is one small person within each of us that never grew up past a certain point. In my view, however, we all have an 18-year-old within us with handicaps acquired at earlier stages of development. We don't stop building the floor just because there are some bricks missing; the ego does not stop growing at the age of two or ten or 12. In fact, the inner being is made up of the sum total of all 18 years. Some years will have handicaps, while others will not. If we insist on using the term 'inner child,' we would have to say that, for every missing brick, we have a different 'inner child.' Therefore, I will reword the original question as, "Can our inner self ever grow up?"

In order for our inner self to grow up completely, we would have to fill in all the holes in our floor. In other words, we would have to shape all those parts of the ego that were never shaped. This is not an easy task, for several reasons. First, as long as there are barriers around the holes, we won't be able to fill them in. Second, just as we cannot see yesterday's child with today's eyes, we cannot teach her with today's values. Third, what is easily shaped in a four-year-old's ego may be extremely difficult, if not impossible, to shape in an adult.

The more fundamental a part of our ego system is, the more difficult it is for us to shape it as adults. Trust, for example, is shaped very early on, in the first two years of life. Confidence in one's intellectual skills, however, is not formed until adolescence. An adult, therefore, will have considerably more difficulty learning to trust than he will gaining confidence in his intellectual ability.

We may never fill in all the voids in our egos. However, when we start removing the barriers and actually seeing the voids for what they are, the growing up process can begin again. Once we can accept that we have needs, the ego defence can be set to rest and we can allow ourselves to be nurtured. Only then can we begin filling in the holes. This process may occupy us for an entire lifetime, and we need to feel okay about that.

If our 18-year old ego were fully developed, what would we be like?

Many people believe that to be 'mature' is to lose youthfulness and spontaneity. In fact, the opposite is true. If a person were to have a fully grown ego—a floor with no missing bricks—he wouldn't have the need for barriers or defences. Without the fear of encountering or falling into a void, he could freely experience every corner of himself. Because he would have no voids in his ego system, he wouldn't feel compelled to hide behind a mask of maturity; he would live in a state of total self-awareness. Such a person would not see himself as being only one age, whether 21, 40 or 55. He would carry with him at all times the awareness of all his ages. Such people are rare.

Does trust play a role in our adult lives?

Trust can be a very dangerous thing. A man once came to see me because his wife had left him for someone else. He was in a state of disbelief; he said, "I trusted her." I asked him what he meant. He replied that he had trusted her to stay with him forever, to be home waiting for him when he returned from work, to always be faithful, to never leave the children, and to take care of him when he got old. I asked him how he showed his wife that he loved, appreciated and valued her. He responded by saying that he was always faithful and that she, of course, knew this.

For this man, trusting his wife meant taking her for granted. He expected her to survive without nurturing and still meet all his needs. He trusted her as a young child would trust his mother: "I'm a good boy (I'm faithful), therefore mommy loves me." His wife, however, felt neither trusted nor loved; she felt used up.

Adult trust differs from infant trust in several important ways. Adult trust involves taking responsibility for ourselves and making a conscious decision whether or not to trust. Many people are unable to make that decision, but instead wait for it to be made for them. In other words, they wait for the other person to *prove* his trustworthiness, which, of course, he will never be able to do to their satisfaction.

An example of adult trust is when we visit a chiropractor and make a decision to trust him based on both his reputation and our previous experiences. Having made that decision, we can then give our bodies over completely to the manipulation. If we do not make that decision to trust, we will resist and, as a result, not benefit from the adjustment.

Unlike infant trust, adult trust is something that must be earned and maintained. Within the context of a close friendship or intimate relationship, the decision to trust is based upon our knowledge and experience of our friend or partner. But unless we are prepared to invest our energy in a relationship, we cannot expect trust to be maintained. If we fail to take responsibility for ourselves and avoid making the decision to trust, we will be unable to truly relax in our relationships. Instead, we will remain on the defensive, always waiting for our partners to let us down.

The man whose wife left him exhibited infant, not adult, trust. Had the relationship been built on a foundation of adult trust, he would have taken responsibility for himself, and then invested his energy in his wife, paying attention to her needs rather than taking her for granted. He could then have made a decision to trust her, feeling confident that she would have his best interests at heart.

The word selfish *is used to describe both the soul's and the tree's drive to grow; isn't selfishness a negative trait?*

It is very important that we distinguish between selfish actions—those taken for the sake of growth and learning, and self-centred actions—those taken for the sake of self-feeding. Whereas on the surface, they may appear to be the same, selfishness works in the service of the ego, while self-centredness works in the service of the ego defence. A selfish act motivates us and moves us forward towards growth, but never enslaves others. A self-centred act makes no forward motion but instead

40

draws energy towards itself. While a selfish person works for survival, a self-centred one gets others to do the work for him. A selfish person takes action to feel secure, whereas a self-centred one depends on others for his security. A selfish person can never be used and a self-centred person always uses.

Self-centred people have given selfishness a bad name. As a result, we are afraid to take action on our own behalf, always putting others' needs before our own. But if we insist on seeing selfishness as a negative, where will we classify love or our instinct for survival?

42

CHAPTER 3

The Flowing Aura

What a drop of seawater is to the oceans of the world, so is the energy egg to the universe. Although it does not contain all the fish, vegetation and ships that populate the oceans, a drop of seawater is, in essence, the same as the oceans. Similarly, an energy egg is, in essence, the same as the universe, even though it does not contain all that is found in the universe. We saw in the first chapter that the energy egg is formed when the soul takes possession of a baby, enveloping the body with its energy or auric field. One of the layers of the energy egg becomes the *flowing* aura, which flows continuously through and around the body. The flowing aura is the bridge between the physical body and the psyche self. In this chapter, we will explore the nature of this bridge.

At the beginning of a person's life, the flowing aura is driven entirely by the soul. As the identity begins to develop, the mind—including the ego system—starts to influence the aura's flow by virtue of its thought process.

Every time we have a thought, the brain is stimulated to produce mind energy. When we think about something or someone outside of ourselves, the mind projects the energy towards the object of our thoughts. This process is called telepathy, which we can define as any movement of information or energy by means of the mind. As the mind drives its thoughts outwards, it enhances the auric flow.

In a healthy person, it takes the aura between seven and nine seconds to flow from the top of the head to the bottom of the feet. From the feet, it continues to flow upwards between the legs and into the base of the body. From there, it travels through the body up to the shoulders, and then increases its speed as it flows through the neck and out the top of the head. The increase of speed is necessary in order for the head and brain to function properly.

Let's look now at the relationship between the flowing aura and the other energies within the physical body. The digestive system, or fuel cell, extracts nutrients from the food we eat and transfers them into the blood. Each organ takes out of the blood those nutrients it requires to produce the energy with which it envelops itself. This energy ensures that the organ functions properly and that it continues to generate new cells.

By itself, the energy around any given organ is inert, clinging to the organ like a gel. When it is activated or vitalized by the auric flow, it becomes fluid. In this state, it is able to energize the organ so that it can function optimally. When the organs of the fuel cell have an abundance of energy, it can be directed to where it is needed, whether that be the brain, the limbs, or the digestive system.

It is because the energy of the auric flow is stronger than that of the energy envelopes that it is able to enhance the organ's functioning. The aura, in effect, raises the energy surrounding the organs to its own vibrational level or frequency. Because the mind influences the auric flow and the quality of the aura, which in turn controls the quality of the body energies and organs, the mind plays a major part in creating the conditions for health or illness.

There are many different attitudes or states of mind, all of which can influence our health. We'll focus on just five examples, each creating a different aura, or auric pattern. Some people have one predominant state of mind, although they will experience others from time to time. Other people shift back and forth between two or more.

The most natural state of mind, and the one which many people aim to achieve, is the loving state of mind. It is the one most likely to promote psychological and physical wellness. The four others we will look at—the angry, caretaking, dormant, and internalizing states of mind—are all associated with varying degrees of psychological and physical difficulties, but only when they become dominant. In that case, they are usually driven by the ego defence. It is normal, however, for people to experience these other states of mind periodically, whether ego defence-driven or not. Anger, for example, may be an appropriate response to discrimination or abuse. Even when a state of mind is ego defence-driven, it can, in some cases, have a positive outcome, such as spiritual growth.

A person with a loving state of mind has a zest for life and is in tune with his environment. He likes to get up in the morning and go to work, he enjoys recreation, and he has respect for himself and others. This person is seldom under stress because he doesn't question the natural order of things. He looks at the rain as a life-giver, rather than an inconvenience.

To those who can sense it, the aura of a loving person feels inviting and warm, and has a gentle, wavy pattern. Its frequency is the most natural. Usually about three inches in thickness, it flows steadily from the top of the head to the bottom of the feet in about eight seconds. Inside this aura, the organs are in their optimum state of wellness. This means that the body is as healthy as it can be, given its own particular genetic makeup and history. From a psychological point of view, there are only pluses to this type of energy.

The loving state of mind comes from the ego or the 'I am.' While a loving person may sometimes respond defensively from the 'I am not' place in the ego system, he will usually return to a predominantly loving state of mind before too long.

Second, we have the angry state of mind. A person with this state of mind carries a chip on his shoulder. He feels that the world is trying to rip him off, believing that anyone who earns more than he does is a thief. He doesn't accept the system in which he lives, and distrusts politicians, law enforcers, bosses—anyone in a position of authority. The person with an angry mind was probably suppressed as a child and not allowed to express himself. He may have been pushed aside or even abused by self-centred parents or older siblings and, as an adult, he tries to get his own back by becoming the bully or the tyrant.

The aura of an angry person feels hot, agitated and even prickly. It is close to the body and more condensed. It takes between seven and nine seconds to travel from the top of the head to the bottom of the feet but, unlike the aura associated with a loving state of mind, its speed is erratic. Because its agitated quality is passed on to the organs, the body's health is adversely affected. The angry person is likely to be afflicted with numerous minor ailments, leading him to complain or blame somebody else. From a psychological point of view, the angry person is a menace to other people, affecting them in a negative way. His auric field not only influences his immediate environment, but may, through a ripple effect, have a more widespread influence. When he is not expressing his anger verbally, it is projected to others through telepathy.

Next, we have the caretaking mind, which, paradoxically, produces an aura with a quality of emptiness or need. Caretaking in itself is often viewed as a positive trait. However, the constant desire to help others often stems from the caretaker's tremendous need for validation. The caretaker shows compassion for the world and everything in it. She cries for the poor rabbit that gets eaten by the fox, unwilling to accept the natural order of life. She is involved in the lives of everyone around her and feels she has to take care of them all: her neighbour whose husband lost his job, the people down the street whose furnace broke down, her unmarried 35-year-old son, and her grown children whom she feels could not manage without her. In the most extreme cases, the caretaking person is the opposite of the loving person. She is very manipulative, contriving to keep people around her so she can take care of them, thereby fostering their dependence upon her.

It is only through this behaviour that she feels important and valued.

The caretaker's aura feels cool and sits close to the body. Because the caretaker is self-centred (contrary to appearances), her mind does not project its energies to the same extent as the loving mind does. Consequently, the aura is drawn inwards and tends to travel more slowly. The caretaker's aura has a quality of need, which has the effect of drawing others towards it, and it may drain the energy of those who are nearby.

As the aura travels through the caretaker's body, its neediness is transferred to the energy envelopes surrounding the organs. As a result, what is essentially an *emotional* need can actually trigger a *physical* response, such as hunger. Because the caretaker cannot genuinely share or give of herself, her aura is unable to adequately stimulate the energy envelopes. Thus, the body will have difficulty healing itself.

The fourth example is the dormant state of mind. This is a very inactive mind—the 'couch potato' of the bunch. Passively allowing himself to be entertained, the person with a dormant mind shows little or no interest in anything that requires effort. He is often very opinionated, using information which derives from other people's labour. His auric flow is extremely slow, creating a very passive energy body in which the organs sit, and his body is prone to numerous minor illnesses.

The most unhealthy state of mind is the internalizing one. The associated aura is close to the body and slow in speed, taking as long as 25 seconds to travel from the top of the head to the bottom of the feet. The aura moves slowly for two reasons: one, because the mind pushes its energies inwards, rather than projecting them; and two, because the large amount of internalized energy lodged within the body blocks the auric flow. Because of the slow speed of the aura, internalizers are often tired and complain of having no energy. The feeling that the aura transmits to others will depend upon the nature of the internalization. Generally we are not attracted to internalizers; because of their preoccupation with themselves, it is as if they are not there. Those who do come in contact with this type of person, however, may feel drained as a result.

The person with an internalizing state of mind is constantly in conflict and frequently troubled by feelings of regret, guilt, self-doubt, inadequacy, resentment or anger. He is always worried about what other people think of him and, as a result, he is often in a defensive state. He is constantly carrying on arguments in his head, in an attempt to justify his behaviour or opinions. He may still be arguing with his mother who has been buried for ten years. He is still upset that he didn't say 'this' rather than 'that' in a discussion that occurred over a month ago. He hates himself for not having taken the opportunity to do something when he had the chance. He may still be angry at himself for getting a speeding ticket weeks ago and, in his mind, he is still offering the policeman rationalizations for his behaviour.

The internalizer feels inadequate and is rarely at peace. In many cases, his feelings of inadequacy are compounded by the fact that he was never allowed to express himself when he was younger. Combine these factors with his preoccupation with the way others see him, and the result is a person who cannot tolerate the possibility that he may have made a mistake. Consequently, he worries about everything he does. He replays scenarios from the past, keeping them alive and emotionally charged, and creates new scenarios in which he revenges himself or otherwise proves himself to be right, all in an attempt to subdue his bad feelings.

Our state of mind at any given time is largely controlled by our ego system. In the loving state of mind, which is compatible with the 'I am,' the ego system is relaxed; in other words, we are not on the defensive. It is easy for us to respond with joy to an experience or event. As we experience joy, our brain is being continually stimulated to produce mind energy and, as we express it, either through laughter or other means, the energy is projected outwards. Once the feeling has subsided, the joyful event becomes a memory which is stored in the mind around the brain. This includes a *memory* of the emotion, but not the emotion itself.

When the ego system has been challenged— if, for example, someone says something that questions our integrity—we may feel anger and wish to express it. The anger we feel in this type of situation is compatible with the 'I am.' The brain is stimulated to produce energy and, as we communicate our anger, it is projected and released. Once the feeling has subsided, provided that there has been some resolution of the conflict, the event becomes a memory stored in the mind around the brain, including a memory of the emotion. The emotions themselves are at rest.

There is an entirely different outcome when a conflict remains unresolved in our minds. If, for example, we are still angry about our speeding ticket because we can't accept that we did something wrong, we won't be able to let go of that anger and it will be internalized. This may be because the situation is similar to old unresolved conflicts relating to authority—conflicts which we may not even remember.

Each time we replay the scenario with the policeman or create new emotionally charged scenarios in which we try to vindicate ourselves, the brain responds by producing new mind energy. Because of the stress generated by these thoughts, the brain has to produce even more energy than usual. But this excess energy has nowhere to go; it is not being projected because we are not communicating with anyone outside of ourselves. Nor is it being used to store the memory of the original scenario. In fact, the energy can't be stored, because it is still alive and emotionally charged.

Because the scenario relates to self, the mind energy produced to replay it is internalized. In other words, it is pushed inwards. The nervous system acts as a conduit, directing the flow of internalized mind energy towards a site in the body where it may be disposed. Sometimes the disposal site is an injured or diseased part of the body that needs additional energy to repair itself. That part of the body now becomes the 'dumping ground' for pools of internalized mind energy or 'secondary mind.'

More often, it is a part of the body which is associated with psychological conflict that becomes a dumping ground for secondary mind. This may be a part about which we feel ashamed or uncomfortable. For example, women who are in conflict about their sexuality may dump internalized mind energy in the reproductive area or the breasts, while men who have bottled up their feelings may dispose of them in the area around the heart.

Because mind energy is of a different frequency than that of the energy envelopes around the organs, it cannot be used to nourish them. As mind energy takes the place of the energy envelopes, the organs will be smothered and have difficulty producing and storing their own energy. Also, because mind energy is stronger and denser than the energy of the aura, it prevents the auric flow from passing through the organs and vitalizing what energy they do have. As a result, cell renewal is hampered and the organ may deteriorate.

Mind energy can also be lodged in other parts of the body, such as the arms and legs, blocking the flow of energy to those areas. Consequently, the limbs may tire easily and, eventually, function will be impaired.

The pockets of internalized mind energy may severely curtail the speed of the auric flow around and through the body. When the aura slows down, it deprives the entire body of the energy it needs to work properly. The brain, which depends upon a powerful auric flow in order to perform at its optimum capacity, is stretched to its limits. The internalized mind energy may slow the aura down to such a degree that normal functioning becomes impossible and, in some cases, serious depression may occur.

In extreme cases, the auric flow can come to a near standstill. If a person whose aura has slowed to such an extent experiences a trauma, the flow can actually be reversed. As a result, the brain does not get the required force of the auric flow, and both physical and psychological functioning are severely disturbed. At this stage, the condition is extremely difficult to rectify, and may manifest itself as manic-depressive illness.

As the bridge between the psyche self and the physical body, the flowing aura is very closely connected with both our mental and physical well-being. Unless the aura is given the attention it deserves, all our tools and procedures for healing will only be partially successful.

Questions

Do we have to be in a loving state of mind all the time in order to stay healthy?

Remember that not all illness is related to our state of mind. Like all other living things, the body is a product of nature and, as such, it may become ill, it will age and, eventually, die. Our state of mind does influence our health in many ways, however. A loving state of mind is the body's best means of resisting illness and healing itself. The internalizing mind is just the opposite; it multiplies our chances of becoming ill and hampers the healing process. A freely flowing aura with no obstructions is our great-est asset when it comes to maintaining a healthy body.

In our society, it is very difficult for people to be in a loving state of mind all the time. Many of us must deal with illness, unemployment, or emotional trauma. Through the media, we hear about abuse, injustice, violence, accidents, poverty and homelessness, and are confronted with the pain these situations bring to other people's lives. We respond with feelings of anger, sadness, fear, grief and, often, helplessness.

So how can we possibly maintain a loving state of mind? We need to begin by realizing that pain and suffering are an integral part of life on this planet, both for humans and animals. Unlike animals, however, who cause pain only through their drive to survive, humans have the capacity for deliberate cruelty. It derives from the nature of the ego system and its all too common voids. But unless we are prepared to take action to prevent or alleviate pain and suffering, no purpose is served by dwelling on it. In fact, in doing so, we only harm ourselves.

Once we accept *what is*, we will no longer expend our energies on complaining about or fighting reality. We may even become angry that we wasted so much time and energy, and this anger may serve to propel us. We will then be able to start forming realistic goals towards changing our present situation. As a result, we will project our energies outwards, away from ourselves, with purpose. This process will naturally bring us into a loving state of mind.

If anger has such a negative effect on our bodies and our environment, why is it sometimes desirable to be angry?

People who periodically get angry should not be confused with those who are in a habitual state of anger and non-acceptance. Anger is a normal response to abuse, injustice or insult, causing us to assert or defend ourselves, and it can be observed as early as infancy. A baby may become angry with the breast for not appearing quickly enough or providing enough milk, at times even striking the mother with its small fist. Children erupt in anger when something is taken away from them.

A mother who loves her child will become very angry when she sees someone harming him. When he harms himself through his own carelessness, she may even become angry at *him.* Her anger is a primal response arising from the desire to protect life. It instills fear in the child, making him hesitant to repeat the action, not because he understands the danger, but because he's afraid of his mother's anger. The female bear also gets very angry if someone comes between her and her cubs. For neither mother is the anger malicious, even though it could drive them both to kill.

As we get older, we are taught to control and even to suppress our normal anger response. When anger is suppressed, however, it can turn into resentment or even hatred. Both of these are negatively focused energies intended to hurt or destroy. Rather than enabling us to express our feelings or attempt to resolve the issue, they may lead us to seek revenge. One of the most damaging consequences of unresolved anger is internalization, which we have discussed earlier.

For these reasons, it's important for us to learn ways of communicating our anger that don't allow our feelings to get the better of us. We need to be able to say, "I am becoming angry," or "That makes me very angry," without having to throw or destroy something, or behave in a manipulative way to get our point across. Once the anger has served its purpose, whether it be to set a boundary, challenge an insult, overcome an obstacle, or rectify an injustice, we can return to a loving state of mind, feeling glad that we have spoken out.

Sometimes we find that our anger does not serve any purpose. There are some situations that we are powerless to change even though we may consider them to be unfair. In these cases, we need to set a limit on how long we want to stay angry. Anger is a force that must be used constructively. Unless we can harness it to our advantage, that force will turn against us.

Do we start to internalize in childhood?

A little boy discovers his penis. It is very intriguing, so he pulls on it, just as he played with his fingers as a baby. He doesn't know it's a 'bad' part until his mother begins to slap his hands saying, "Don't touch, that's bad." In his mind, the penis becomes bad because, whenever he touches it, his mother gets angry.

A little girl is constantly being told, "Don't play with it," "Don't touch that," "Put your legs together," "Don't lift up your dress," or "Keep your panties on." The message she is getting is that her genitals are not nice; in fact, because her interest in them makes her mother so unhappy, they must be very bad.

While children are often complimented for their appearance, many are taught that their natural bodily functions and sexual organs are unclean and shameful. These children are getting the message that they are not okay, leaving a void in the ego which later becomes a need for acceptance. It is here that the ego defence comes into play. In order for the child to feel okay, he must reject that part of the body that his mother views as 'bad.' This causes him to be in conflict about his own body. The foundation is laid for sexual difficulties in adulthood and internalization in the reproductive area once puberty is reached. Energies internalized as a result of conflict over sexuality become part of the overall psyche and remain with the person throughout his life.

Diagnostic imagery, which enables us to view energy lodged in the body, shows a typical pattern of internalization. Children of both sexes who are in conflict tend to internalize energy in the groin and eventually the legs. As girls become women and begin to see themselves as sexual beings, internalized mind usually settles in and around the reproductive organs and the breasts. Even though these women may have forgotten what they were told as children, the knowledge that certain parts are 'bad' is still present in their subconscious minds. As well as lacking validation for their identity as females, they may also be ashamed by the onset of menstruation.

One might expect men to internalize in their genitals as well, but we have rarely found this to be the case. Instead, we find that they tend to internalize in the chest cavity, specifically around the heart. It is often the case that little boys are not allowed to show how they feel. They are expected to be tough, or they risk being viewed as sissies. They are discouraged not only from touching themselves, but also from being *in touch with* themselves. It is well known that the chest is a symbol of male dominance and pride. When feelings are forced to be withheld, the chest becomes no more than a shield of armour covering a fragile heart. This may be the reason why, in men, internalized energies collect around the heart.

Today, women are subject to similar constraints on their feelings, particularly those who work in the business world. For some, there can be the additional stresses of single parenthood, such as lack of emotional support and the stigma of being without a partner. The few woman I have seen with internalized energies around the heart were career women in traditionally male-dominated fields who had to compete directly with their male colleagues.

If we try to take control of our thoughts, do we end up losing the ability to be spontaneous, and do we close ourselves off from the psyche?

Controlling our thoughts does not necessarily mean suppressing them. What it does mean is, first, becoming aware of our unproductive thought patterns—worrying, wishing and wanting, regretting, or otherwise spinning our wheels—and then deciding how we really want to use our minds. Do we want them to wander without direction or continually replay troubling scenarios, producing nothing but a lot of anxiety and a surplus of mind energy? Or do we want to focus them by paying closer attention to what we are doing?

If we choose the latter, we are not suppressing our thoughts, we are actually opening up our minds. A focused mind is a questioning and receptive one. It is a law of the psyche that, when we have a desire to know, we are automatically open to receive. A new thought or awareness will never enter a mind that is always arguing or otherwise preoccupied with itself.

Does the soul ever stop driving the auric flow entirely?

From the moment the soul takes possession of the infant, it is continuously driving the aura. Throughout our lives, however, the mind exerts an influence over the auric flow and can, in exceptional circumstances, stop it altogether. So even though the soul is always driving the aura, the obstacles created by our minds (especially live memories stored within the body) may hamper its flow to some degree.

Is the body always in the middle of the energy egg?

Recall that an energy egg is formed when the soul takes possession of a baby, and that it is the principal part of the total psyche being. Of the many layers that make up the energy egg, the one that is closest to the body, but not *of* the body, is the flowing aura.

Under normal circumstances, the flowing aura is in the middle of the energy egg, and the body is centred within the flowing aura. Sometimes, however, the aura will shift in relation to the body, but the body will remain centred within the energy egg as a whole. At other times, the whole energy egg, including the aura, will shift in relation to the body. In these cases, it is said that the body is off-centre, but what is really meant is that the psyche is off-centre in relation to the body.

When the body is in the middle of the aura, the aura flows evenly around all sides of it. As the aura flows back into the body, it lines up with the body's centre, just in front of the spine. When the body is not in the middle of the aura, the centre of the aura might be as far over as the outer perimeter of the body.

The aura appears to have a greater flow on the dominant side (based on the person's handedness), visible at the top and side of the head. This may give the impression that we are off-centre, yet we are not.

There are many circumstances that may cause the psyche to become off-centre in relation to the body. If there is an energy obstruction at some point within the body, for example, the increased resistance in that area causes the aura to shift its path in order to bypass the obstruction. In a case like this, the aura—but not necessarily the whole energy egg—will be off-centre in relation to the body.

Another example is when someone has pain in one side of his body and he wants to remove himself from it. Though his body cannot move away, his psyche—including the aura—may shift away from the source of pain, leaving him off-centre in relation to his body.

A third example is when a person is unhappy with her relationship and, while sleeping with her partner, shifts away from him psychically. Similarly, a person who is very dominant and possessive can pull his partner's psyche towards him. The psyche can also move off-centre in relation to the body when we want to escape from ourselves.

In all of these examples, a person whose psyche has shifted in relation to his body may have the feeling of being 'beside himself.'

CHAPTER 4

Psychic Communication

We are all communicators. We communicate through speaking and writing and, often unconsciously, through our facial expressions and other body language. What we may not know, however, is that we are constantly sending and receiving information psychically. There are basically two means through which we communicate psychically: mental telepathy and auric sensing. Mental telepathy involves the transfer of thought by mind, while auric sensing involves the transfer of information through our energy egg or auric field.

Whenever we have a thought, the brain is stimulated to produce a small amount of energy. When that thought relates to something or someone outside of ourselves, the energy automatically travels towards that object or person, and a psychic link is formed. This link is like a wire over which information flows from one person to the other. The flow of information via psychic link is called mental telepathy.

Here is an example of mental telepathy that most people have experienced. You are thinking about a friend whom you haven't seen for a long time. The phone rings. Your friend is on the line, asking how you are. You reply: "What a coincidence, I was just thinking about you!" In fact, this might not have been a coincidence at all; it is quite possible that through mental telepathy, you thought of your friend before the call. A little bit of inquiry may determine who started thinking about whom first. You may have thought about your friend first, prompting him to make the phone call. Alternatively, your friend may have been thinking about you while deciding to make the phone call and his thought travelled to you even before he began dialling. When the phone rang, you were already thinking about him.

We don't receive every thought that is projected towards us, however. Whether or not information is received will depend upon the degree to which we are preoccupied at the time. We are more likely to be in a receptive state of mind while attending to a routine task than while reading or trying to solve a problem.

Let's look at another example of mental telepathy. Two people are talking on the telephone. Tricia is telling her friend Jason that she is going to Italy and will be visiting Milan. Jason has been to Milan and was very impressed with certain sights. As Tricia is talking about her travel plans, Jason is visualizing some of the wonderful places he visited. Later, when Tricia is visiting these same places in Milan, she has the feeling she's been there before, like a sense of *déjà vu*. She may feel a bit confused and perhaps wonder if there is something to the theory of past lives that she has recently heard about.

Without knowing it, Tricia had received Jason's mental images of the places in Milan that he visualized during their conversation. Those images travelled psychically between the two minds. When Tricia went to Milan, she was already carrying Jason's images of the city in her mind.

There are many examples of mental telepathy in everyday life. Mothers and their infants, for example, often communicate psychically with each other. A mother can often sense at a distance that her child is uncomfortable, unless she is preoccupied with something else. If she is in a receptive state of mind, she may pick up the baby's discomfort even before he starts crying. Alternatively, she might be wondering whether her baby is okay, thereby reaching out psychically and creating a link. This allows her to become aware of her infant's discomfort.

Another example is the woman who is waiting for her partner to return home from work and, as he turns his car into the driveway, she can already sense that he had a rough day at the office. There are two possible explanations for this. The first is that, upon hearing the car in the driveway, the woman reaches out psychically to her partner and is able to sense his state of mind. The second is that her partner, who is in need of consolation, is looking forward to being taken care of.

In auric sensing, the second type of psychic communication, the outer shell of our auric field or energy egg acts like a skin or membrane, receiving information or impressions from its environment. This psychic tool is part and parcel of the human and animal survival kit, helping us to identify and avoid dangerous situations.

Auric information transfer is a type of auric sensing in which two people's auras communicate by touching. This is what is happening when we are standing beside another person and begin to feel anxious for no obvious reason. If we become conscious of our anxiety, we may wonder what is going on, perhaps not realizing that we are picking up someone else's state of mind. We may even find an excuse to walk away, after which we will probably start to feel better.

Small children and animals have a great ability to sense the auric field of an individual who is nearby, just by virtue of their survival instinct. Subconsciously, they are always seeking to identify compatibility or incompatibility; this is how they protect themselves from danger. Psychic law states that if you have a question, you are open to receiving information. Because children and animals are seeking information about their safety, their psychic senses are automatically on the alert, like the whiskers of a cat.

For example, a visitor arrives at your home and your pet dog begins walking towards him. The dog stops about three feet away from him, as though an invisible barrier stands in its way. It backs off, turns away, and growls. Moments later, when the visitor approaches your four-year-old daughter, she runs to hide behind you. You feel embarrassed and tell her to behave nicely, completely ignoring her feelings. You probably didn't notice that the dog and the child acted in a similar fashion, both sensing their incompatibility with the stranger.

A month later, when you find out that the visitor wasn't the nice person you had thought him to be, the dog will be given credit for having sensed this immediately. The child's response, on the other hand, is more likely to have been forgotten. But both she and the dog were receiving information through their psychic senses—their minds' cat whiskers—and both reacted automatically. Both felt uncomfortable. Neither made a judgment; they merely sensed an incompatibility and reacted accordingly.

Young children continually use this psychic tool, the 'cat whiskers.' By the time we reach adulthood, however, most of us have lost the ability to use it. This is because, as children, we are forced to cross our psychic barriers and interact with incompatible people time and time again, without regard for our discomfort. Not surprisingly, this auric sensing ability is eventually suppressed in most people. Also, in our relatively protected modern society, we rarely require this tool for survival. For these two reasons, most adults do not consciously 'listen' or respond to psychic impressions.

Even though most adults are no longer listening for psychic cues, or trying to determine whether they are safe, the same signals are still impacting on the outer layer of the energy egg. In fact, we do respond to these signals, although our responses are mostly unconscious. This is shown in the following examples of another type of auric sensing.

You've been invited to someone's home for the first time. You arrive feeling a little unsure of yourself, so your psyche is open to receiving impressions. Very soon, however, you begin to feel at ease and are able to relax and enjoy your visit. On another occasion, you arrive at someone's home, again not knowing what to expect. After a short period of time, you start feeling uncomfortable and you have a strong urge to leave. In both cases, you have picked up the ambient energy of the house with the outer layer of your auric field. In the first case, you felt compatible with your environment and, therefore, at ease; in the second, you felt incompatible and, therefore, ill at ease. But in both cases, you were probably unaware that your feelings were related to the energy you picked up with your aura.

Here's another example: You are visiting some friends whom you know very well and in whose home you have always felt very comfortable. As soon as you enter the house, however, you sense a difference, and wonder if something is wrong. You ask your friends what's been happening and they confide that they have just had a major argument. Again, you probably didn't realize that you had picked up these impressions psychically.

In all these examples, information in the form of impressions or feelings is picked up by the outer layer of the auric field.

For psychic readers, auric information transfer is the source of a great deal of information about our past and present. There is nothing mysterious about this. When a reader sits beside or across a table from us, his auric field is in contact with ours. Because we come to him wanting answers, we automatically open ourselves psychically. This establishes a psychic channel through which information about us can be accessed by the reader. Auric information transfer is a powerful tool for the reader, along with other sources of information such as body language, facial expression and structure, and the palms of our hands.

A related skill which some readers use is called psychometry. The reader will ask for an object, such as a ring or other piece of jewellery, preferably one containing a gemstone. Holding the object in his hand, he is able to 'tune in' to its energies and gather various kinds of information about us. He may get a sense of how we walk, talk, feel or behave and will likely be able to detect our predominant state of mind. He may even receive impressions about us through mental images. By itself, psychometry is a powerful tool for obtaining information about a person; it is even more powerful when combined with auric information transfer.

How do crystals and metals come to acquire information about us? We have seen in earlier chapters that, as the aura flows around and through the body, it comes to mirror the mind. Our attitudes and feelings—in fact, everything about us—are contained within the auric flow. Any jewellery we wear is enveloped by the aura and takes on its vibrational frequency, although it may take a year or longer before it comes to carry our history within itself. Crystals and some metals will retain these energy patterns almost indefinitely, unless they are altered by a stronger energy.

In many cases, a reader will use information gained through auric information transfer or psychometry in combination with his knowledge of human nature to make educated guesses about our future. Occasionally, he may be right. More often than not, his predictions do not materialize. Some readers, however, do have a genuine capability for precognition. Those who have this fine psychic channel, as well as the appropriate skills to translate and present what they perceive in a responsible way, can be very helpful advisers.

Whether we realize it or not, psychic communication is taking place all the time, through auric information transfer and telepathy. Even when we are silent and have nothing to say, and even when we are asleep, we are communicating psychically. We may hold back our words, but we cannot keep from revealing our state of mind.

Questions

Of what benefit is it to have a psychic reading?

Throughout the history of most cultures, people have consulted 'the wise one'—the shaman, the elder, and so on—for advice. Kings, queens, statesmen and politicians have all been known to seek the help of psychic advisers, including astrologers, in dealing with their extraordinary and sometimes overwhelming responsibilities.

Many people today visit psychic advisers, some simply for entertainment, and others because of a genuine need for guidance in dealing with a particular situation or making a decision. A psychic reading can sometimes be of tremendous benefit. Psychic advisers are similar in some ways to personal counsellors, but they may be able to home in on a person's problem more quickly, using whatever psychic skills they have. They may be sensitive to auric information transfer, skilled in psychometry, or even gifted in clairvoyance or precognition. In some cases, a psychic adviser may also receive spiritual help.[*]

It's important to realize, however, that a psychic reading is only an aid. Too often people become so dependent on readers that they end up being 'psychic slaves.' They may fool themselves into thinking they're just looking for entertainment, but in many cases, their need goes deeper. Their underlying reason may be to have their problems solved for them, or even to get someone's undivided attention. If a reader is unaware of the client's motivation in coming for a reading, it makes her job more difficult. Many of us go to readers because we have a

---

[*] See Willemsen (forthcoming)

problem, yet we pretend that we are going just for entertainment. We withhold information about why we have come, expecting the reader to use psychic means to find out. This is like going to a doctor and refusing to say where it hurts.

Just as we are sometimes less than honest about our needs as a client, readers can also make false claims about their abilities. An unprincipled reader may prey on her client's underlying need, offering him a shred of hope by suggesting that there is the possibility of relief in the immediate future, whether it be through a letter, an encounter with a stranger, or some other event. If she goes on to tell him that she may have more information for him the following month, he will probably feel compelled to return. When he does return, again for the sake of 'entertainment,' he is lured back for yet another visit with the promise of something more next time. If we put our faith in readers such as these—'sellers of hope'—we risk becoming psychic slaves.

How can we tell whether or not we are dealing with a true psychic adviser? First of all, a true psychic adviser will not spend a lot of time telling you things about your past and asking for confirmation. Nor will she inquire about your date of birth, unless she is preparing a detailed astrological reading. She may suggest that you return in eight to ten months, but will not encourage you to keep coming back. A true psychic adviser will want to know why you have come for help, so that she can focus on the area of concern. She is not interested in playing games; she has no need to prove that she is psychic.

The psychic adviser may ask to hold an object belonging to you, such as a ring which you have worn for a long time. She may even take hold of your hand or study your eyes. In these and other ways, she will attempt to get in tune with who you are. If you're asking for help solving a problem, she may enter a kind of trance state, during which she will suggest some options and what their outcomes might be. She will never make the decision for you. Following the reading, she may offer to discuss certain aspects of it if she feels this would be of benefit.

Can anyone learn to become a reader?

It all depends on what kind of a reader you want to be. If you want to learn to read cards, tea leaves or palms, no psychic skills are necessary. They are essential, however, if you want to become a psychic reader (a psychometrist, for example) or a clairvoyant. We often do not distinguish between these categories.

There are books available from which anyone can learn to read tarot cards, playing cards, palms or even tea leaves. Because the cards and the teacup are handled by the client, his psyche will influence the way the cards fall on the table or the shapes are formed by the tea leaves in the cup. The distribution of lines in the palm of a hand is also determined by the psyche. With practice, we can learn to interpret these signs.

To become a psychometrist or a clairvoyant, we have to develop psychic skills. Psychometrists use touch to pick up impressions from an object, while clairvoyants perceive through psychic means alone. Although people who have these psychic capabilities are considered by many to be gifted, both psychometry and clairvoyance can be learned, just like any other skill. As with other skills, though, not everyone has an aptitude for them and even those who do must practise a great deal. While we can learn to read cards or tea leaves on our own, learning psychometry requires the cooperation of other people. They must allow you to practise on their rings and wristwatches and then tell you how accurate you were in your reading. In the process, they will probably have to reveal personal information about themselves.

This brings us to an interesting issue, that of readers who give unsolicited advice. When we meet with them socially, these people may begin to share what they are seeing or feeling about us, and may go so far as to give us advice on a matter we hadn't asked them about. Unless we ask for a reading, thus giving the reader permission to enter our personal space, a reading and the unsolicited advice which comes with it should be seen as interference. A serious reader would consider this behaviour to be inappropriate.

To get back to the original question: yes, we can learn to become readers. But it's important to ask what our purpose is in wanting to learn. Often, people who are troubled have a desire to help others, like the 'caretaker' in the last chapter. The caretaker is primarily interested in satisfying his own need, although he may not be aware of it. In fact, he may unintentionally do more harm than good by giving a reading. Within the psychic realm there is a very fine line between reality and fantasy and, if the reader's desire to help is based on a need for approval or gratification, he is more likely to cross that line. In some cases, the reading may become a reflection of that need. This could be dangerous for the client, particularly if she looks to the reader for advice.

Psychic skills are not playthings. The psychic has to take responsibility for his reading and for its impact on the client. It is irresponsible for a psychic reader to place the onus on cards, tea leaves or any spiritual help he may receive.

If jewellery can hold information about its owner, can it affect another person?

Yes. This is not only true of jewellery, but of many items which are made out of metal or stone, as well as mirrors and pictures. When these objects have been in someone's possession for an extended period of time, they take on the characteristics of that person's psyche. If you wear a piece of someone else's jewellery or come into contact with an object that belonged to him, you will be affected by his energy, just as you would be through auric information transfer.

I once encountered a woman who became sick to her stomach whenever she put on a ring that had belonged to her husband's mother. When she removed the ring, her stomach would stop bothering her. When I took the ring in my hand, I also got a sick feeling and a terrible pain in my stomach. She asked if I could 'clean' the ring so she could continue to wear it. After I neutralized its energy, it no longer gave her any discomfort.

On another occasion, a forty-year old man came to see me, telling me that, a year earlier, his life had begun to take a turn for the worse. My attention was drawn to a ring he was wearing. I asked him about it and he told me he found it at an estate sale and had been wearing it for about a year. As soon as I held it, I felt the urge to throw it away as far as possible; it made me feel very uncomfortable. I strongly suggested that he get rid of the ring. He did, and his life started turning around almost immediately; a business venture, which he subsequently became involved in, brought him success.

In another example, all the members of a family suddenly began to develop headaches in their home. They checked the gas line for leaks and found none, nor could they find any other explanation. I asked if they had recently acquired something new for their house. They said no. When I went to visit the house, everything seemed all right until I walked into the upstairs hallway and suddenly felt a pain on the right side of my head. Turning my head to the right, I saw an old mirror hanging on the wall. I asked them how long they'd had it and they told me they'd acquired it recently. After thinking about it, they realized that they had bought the mirror just before the headaches began. I don't know if their headaches ever cleared up; they were reluctant to get rid of the mirror, and I didn't meet with them again. Nevertheless, I felt strongly that it was the cause of their problem.

Photographs, too, are a powerful storehouse of energy. When a person is photographed, the light that bounces off his body is influenced by his psyche. Both a visual image of the person and an image of his energy frequency are transferred onto the negative. This is consistent with certain aboriginal peoples' belief that, when we take their photograph, we also take a part of their soul.

As an example of this, I was called to the home of a couple who told me that they felt uncomfortable about something in their house, but could not pin it down. Whenever their son visited, he too would comment on the unpleasant feeling, and as a result, was a reluctant visitor. The family felt that there was something in the house that didn't belong, and they even wondered if it could be a spirit. When I arrived in their home, I walked slowly through the house. In the small den, I began to feel heavy and quite uncomfortable. My eyes were drawn to a large photograph of an old woman, which was hanging on the wall in a very ornate frame. The closer I came to the photograph, the more I became convinced that it was the source of my discomfort. I was told that the woman in the photograph was a relative who had been very much disliked. Because it was an old photograph in an antique frame, however, the family had decided to keep it. They were almost angry with me when I advised them to get rid of their family heirloom. So I suggested instead that they put the picture somewhere outside the house for a while. They agreed to store it inside an old chicken coop. I also suggested that they play calming music day and night for a period of time so that the energy frequency in the home would gradually change to a more serene one.

A month later the family reported that they were feeling much better in the house, and that they had almost forgotten about the picture in the chicken coop. The woman told me that when she went to check on it, she felt nauseated as soon as she entered the chicken coop. She knew then that the picture had been responsible for the bad feeling in the house. After that, the family didn't hesitate to get rid of it.

Is it possible to remove someone's energy from a piece of jewellery?

It is not possible to remove energy from a piece of jewellery, only the information it holds. This is achieved by transforming or neutralizing the energy. A piece of jewellery—a ring, for example—that has been worn by one person for a period of time will take on the same energy pattern as that of the person's aura. In order to neutralize it, we need to introduce a stronger energy field. (This is not unlike neutralizing the magnetic strip on a credit card with another magnet.) We begin by building up a large amount of energy within ourselves through a meditative exercise or some other mental discipline. This energy must be strong enough to overcome the energy pattern in the ring, which may have taken many years to develop. We then focus all the energy into one hand, which we use to 'clean' or neutralize the ring. We need to stay highly focused until this process is complete; otherwise, the energy pattern in the ring could affect us. It can sometimes feel like a battle of wills. To be successful in 'cleaning' the ring, our state of mind has to remain neutral. In other words, we need to focus with purpose but without expectation. Some people with a particularly high energy frequency are able to clean a piece of jewellery with less effort than others.

Metal rings can also be cleaned by being melted down. During this process, the properties of the metal are momentarily altered, and the energies are neutralized.

When there is a gem set in the ring, it may be more difficult to change the energy pattern. This is because gems have a much stronger energy within them to begin with. Consequently, gems take on the aura's energy pattern more slowly than metal but, by the same token, they will retain that pattern much longer.

Generally, we should not wear someone else's jewellery or crystal unless we know and feel comfortable about that person.

How is clairvoyance used in psychic readings or psychic communication?

A person with clairvoyant abilities can perceive things beyond the range of the five senses. There are many types of clairvoyance, each corresponding to different objects of extra sensory perception. These include objects at a distance or concealed from sight, energies of the psyche, and spirits (that is, beings without physical substance.) Those who are able to perceive spirits are sometimes able to communicate with them as well.

The 'third eye,' often considered to be the seat of psychic and paranormal powers, is a highly developed clairvoyant channel. Thought to be associated with the pineal gland in the brain, it is located in the centre of the forehead just above the eye-brows. The awakening of the third eye often involves extreme discomfort or even pain. Although it may open spontaneously for a period of time, it usually takes many years of meditative exercises for this to occur.

The third eye can be used in many different ways. It can help us transport our thoughts or energy from one place to another, enabling us to communicate at a distance. It can amplify and direct energy from one point to another in order to facilitate healing. In certain psychic disciplines, it can be used to make changes to the body such as spinal adjustments, even at a considerable distance. The third eye can also be used for diagnostic imagery, a process which allows us to view the skeleton, the nervous system, the soft tissue, the auric flow and the energies of the physical body (including internalized mind energy) in order to determine the cause of a problem.

The third eye is a very powerful tool and as such, it has the potential to be misused. With an open third eye, one is able to influence the psyche of another person—and not necessarily for the better. Psychic abilities are not reserved for those who intend to use them responsibly.

When activating the third eye, it is essential that we are in a non-emotional, psychologically neutral state of mind. Otherwise, the person whom we are trying to help may, instead, be harmed.

Can people communicate through dreams?

Most dreams are a manifestation of one's subconscious mind. Some, however, are psychic communications coming from outside of ourselves. Even those of us who are not normally open to such communications are able to receive them in their dreams. This is because we are in a very receptive state of mind while we sleep. These communications can come from both people and spirits.

You may wake up one morning, for example, having had a dream that a close friend was anxious to tell you something. When you telephone her, you find out that she has recently suffered a head injury and is recovering in hospital. Many people have had the experience of seeing a close relative in a dream who tells them, "Don't be upset, I'm okay," only to find out shortly afterwards that the person has just died.

Dream mediumship, a process whereby one actually seeks out communication with people or spirits through one's dreams, may also be practised as a psychic discipline.

Can we become aware of our own energy or auric fields?

Many people are aware of their own energy fields but don't realize it. You might walk into a room, feel uncomfortable and decide to leave.

85

Without being aware of it, you have actually responded to information received through your own energy field. Another example is the feeling of needing space around yourself, of feeling crowded. This feeling is unrelated to claustrophobia; again, it is a communication from your own energy field.

Through meditative disciplines, you can learn to amplify your energy field, becoming acutely aware of your outer boundary. Gradually, you come to feel that you *are* that energy egg—a molecule of the universe—with your body floating in the middle of it. You will have a sense that there is neither up nor down and you may see everything surrounding your energy field simultaneously, in one picture. Yet you will be unable to translate or make sense of what you see because you are no longer connected to your body. You can remain in that awareness for a moment or a longer period of time, feeling 'as one.'

Is it possible to learn to see or feel the flowing aura and other energies of the psyche?

Before we can learn to see anything in the psyche, we have to first believe it is there. This seems to run counter to the popular notion that seeing is believing. However, if we really think about it, this notion does not hold up very well in everyday life. In fact, we are seldom able to recognize or acknowledge new information or ideas that run counter to our beliefs.

In order to learn to see or feel the energies of the psyche, we have to begin by *behaving* as though they were a reality. This is not quite the same as believing, which usually involves blind acceptance. It's more like the idea of a working hypothesis in science. In order to prove the existence of something unseen—radio waves, for example—scientists first hypothesize its existence and then set up an appropriate experiment to test their hypothesis. Similarly, with the psyche, once we assume that it exists, we can then make appropriate observations and gather data. We usually begin by learning to detect subtle differences in the feel of the energies and, eventually, we develop the ability to interpret their significance. If, on the other hand, we begin by believing that they don't exist, we are unlikely to make any observations because we will ignore what we do see or feel.

One major obstacle in the development of psychic awareness is the failure to recognize the difference between fantasy and psychic reality. Because we are so accustomed to sensing with our physical faculties, it is difficult to know if what we are sensing psychically is real. The principal requirement is honesty, which begins with an understanding of why we want to learn to sense in the first place. It also involves asking ourselves how badly we need to feel something. Do we have something to prove? Are we in competition with someone? Before we start sensing psychically, it's important that we deal with these issues, or at least be aware of them. Psychic awareness involves setting aside our wants and pre-conceptions and being prepared to make mistakes; if we are afraid to make a mistake, we can never be totally open and responsive. Ultimately, it is our ego systems that will determine how quickly we learn to discriminate between psychic reality and fantasy.

There is also the matter of aptitude. Everyone can learn to paint, but the degree of talent varies widely. It is the same with the psyche; everyone who is prepared to invest time and effort can obtain *some* degree of psychic awareness. Even those who have innate ability, however, still require many years of practice to perfect their skills.

CHAPTER 5

Health
and Healing

The awareness and acknowledgment of energy as a factor in human health goes back as far as the oldest healers. They knew that the body was the true healer and they were only facilitators. They used all the herbs nature made available to them, together with their knowledge of the psyche, to provide comfort, facilitate healing, and promote wellness. They understood the importance of the psyche in health and illness because they knew that the body lives within and responds to the psyche. Although this way of healing had been accepted throughout history, in recent years it has all but been destroyed.

Science and technology have altered our relationship with the natural order of life. Horses have given way to cars, natural remedies to aspirin, and awareness of the psyche to scientific hypotheses. In our eagerness to embrace new technologies, we expose ourselves to a multitude of risks. While we used to move around at six kilometres an hour, occasionally bumping into a tree, we now encase ourselves in metal containers and propel ourselves at 100 kilometres an hour. We may still bump into the same tree, but instead of getting bruises or abrasions, we re-arrange our entire skeleton. To add insult to injury, our bodies now have to cope with such toxins as pesticides, herbicides, antibiotics, hormones and other food additives.

When we become ill, we no longer look to herbs and energies to restore our bodies to health. We rely solely on the tools of modern medicine to alleviate our suffering. Our primary concern is to repair the body as quickly as possible, so that we can get on with our lives. Every day is a dollar, after all. The repair often involves suppressing the symptoms, and hoping that the problem goes away. If it doesn't go away quickly, because something is really wrong with the body, we get scared and our fear of dying is awakened. We often resort to extreme measures— sometimes going so far as to remove the part of the body that is misbehaving—believing those measures to be necessary for our survival. This method of dealing with physical illness reflects a particularly Western perspective, one from which we view ourselves as physical beings first and foremost. We believe that we *are* our bodies. Because we are unaware of the reality of the psyche, our attempts at healing focus only on the physical symptoms of our illness. Our treatment is confined to the body even though it is often the psyche that needs our attention.

To fully understand illness and its origins, we need to be aware of the relationship between the physical body, the body psyche (energies associated with the physical body) and the mind. Both the body and the mind can become ill, and in both cases this will influence the body psyche.

There are two principal types of illness: physical and psychological (or emotional). The first consists of the breakdown of a body part due to wear and tear, infectious disease, environmental pollutants, misuse or abuse, injury, or other trauma. The second type of illness is usually related to problems of the mind or the ego system, such as lack of confidence or self-esteem, family or relationship problems, lack of purpose or direction, or psychological trauma.

Psychological illness causes a disturbance in the energies of the body (the body psyche); physical illness may do the same. Both have the potential to deplete those energies, thus interfering with the

91

body's ability to heal itself. The body psyche can also be affected by spinal misalignment, inadequate rest or nutrition, lack of physical exercise, and physical or emotional stress. The depletion of the body psyche may eventually manifest itself as a breakdown within the physical body.

There are three types of healing. The first two roughly correspond to the two types of illness discussed above. One of these is physical healing, in which changes are made to the body by physical means in order to rid it of disease or otherwise restore it to health. Some examples of this are surgery, drug therapy, physiotherapy, chiropractic, therapeutic massage, nutritional therapy and herbs. The second type of healing is psychological, involving treatments aimed at improving the health of the mind or ego system. These include counselling, psychotherapy and, in some cases, meditative exercises. Psychological methods may also play an indirect role in the restoration of physical health. (Some health practitioners believe that illnesses relating to the mind are actually physiological in nature and treat them accordingly, often with drug therapy.)

The third type is psychic healing, which can be used for the treatment of both physical and psychological illness. In both cases, the goal of psychic healing is to restore balance to the body psyche. Treatments of the psyche can take the form of energy manipulation and transfer, meditative exercises and, in some cases, counselling. In this chapter, we will concentrate primarily on energy manipulation and transfer.

Energy manipulation is the most basic and natural mode of psychic healing. It is the form of healing a mother uses as she strokes her baby's body in order to alleviate his distress or discomfort. Babies quickly stop crying in response to their mother's stroking. But what is actually happening? One could argue that the baby likes getting his mother's attention and enjoys the touch and, therefore, stops crying. That may sometimes be the case. But other things are happening as well. The mother is having loving thoughts about her crying infant as she strokes his body. Her focus on soothing the baby causes a buildup of energy around the hand. In this way, her hand becomes an instrument of the psyche, capable of manipulating the baby's energy field (including the flowing aura) and settling its disturbance. It doesn't matter whether the baby's energies were disturbed by his crying or whether his crying was caused by the disturbance; as the energies are manipulated, they relax and the baby comes to feel at ease.

There may be another explanation for what is happening when the mother strokes her baby. Suppose that the baby is short of energy for some reason. Perhaps he hasn't been sleeping well and has been crying a lot, or he has used up a lot of energy digesting his food. In either case, the lack of energy causes him to feel uncomfortable. As the mother strokes him, her energy automatically flows through her hand and into his body. This causes the baby's energy level to build up again and he begins to feel comfortable.

Whichever of these two explanations best describes what is happening between the mother and her infant, in neither case does the mother actually *heal* the infant. What occurs is merely a manipulation or transfer of energy. If healing does take place, it is accomplished by the infant's own body. All the mother does is supply the needed energy; the baby's body takes care of the rest. This process is often referred to as "the laying on of hands," and it is practised all over the world. It can be used to restore energy to the body as a whole or to any part of it. Within a religious setting, other factors, such as prayer, can play a role in the laying on of hands.[*]

Any organ or other body part can become depleted of energy if it is unable to draw from the blood those ingredients it requires to maintain its own energy envelope. This can be the result of improper nutrition, poor digestion, or some other ailment which prevents it from replenishing its energy stores. When an organ is in need of energy, the person will feel pain. This is the body's way of alerting him to the problem.

---

[*] See Willemsen (forthcoming)

In order for the organ to heal itself, it may require some outside help, such as medication or nutritional therapy. If neither of these methods is effective, then the laying on of hands may succeed in providing energy to the ailing organ, thereby giving it the opportunity to heal. If the pain disappears, it means that the organ received the energy it needed to begin healing itself.

Energy transfer can also work in combination with other kinds of treatment. For example, it can play a major part in the success or failure of a surgical operation. Surgery is a traumatic event for the body, but the trauma within the psyche begins long before the actual operation takes place. Because the psyche is designed to maintain life, it is placed under threat whenever physical illness occurs. Together with a fear of pain, there is always the fear of dying, whether it is a conscious or subconscious fear. Worry about the operation robs the body of considerable energy at a time when it needs as much as possible. Worry can bring on other changes as well, such as disruptions in eating habits or digestion, and an inability to relax or even sleep. All of these disruptions slowly deplete the body's energy reserves. By the time the operation takes place, the body may have little energy left to heal itself and recovery may be slow. Sometimes, even after a supposedly successful operation, the patient dies for some unknown reason. In these cases, it is possible that, due to a

Don't Water the Stick: The Path of the Psyche

total depletion of energy, the system has gone into a kind of psychic shock, leading to heart failure.

Energy transfer through the laying on of hands may be extremely helpful to a person who is going to have surgery. Besides helping the body to build its energy reserves, it may also help indirectly to reduce anxiety and fear. If the person begins to feel more energetic, he is more likely to feel confident in his body's ability to undergo the stresses of surgery and recovery. Family members and friends who are physically healthy, have a positive outlook, and are well rested may help the patient by touching, stroking, holding, or being near him prior to the operation, in order to send him energy. After the operation, it can also be beneficial to the patient if they lay their hands on his shoulder, head or stomach.

The same effect can be achieved over a distance, in the following way. A person focuses his mind on the patient and, by visualizing him, she mentally projects her energy through loving and caring thoughts. This is an example of the transfer of energy by means of telepathy. It can be done before, during and after the operation. The results are usually a shorter than expected recovery time and fewer complications.

In addition to the laying on of hands and telepathy, the transfer of energy can also occur through the interaction of two auric fields. In the following example, however, the energy which flows from a healthy person to a less healthy one does not have a positive outcome.

A woman feels obliged to visit her elderly aunt who is in hospital recovering from an operation. It is a rainy day and she has to park two blocks away from the hospital. She hasn't finished an assignment which is due the next day, and she resents having to take time out to visit someone whom she doesn't particularly like. When she sits down beside her aunt, she is very irritable, but she smiles nonetheless and pretends she is glad to be there.

Her aunt, who has just received a hip replacement two days earlier, is quite tired, not yet having recovered her energy after the operation. But she is glad of the company and, when her niece has to leave twenty minutes later, she is sorry to see her go. Her niece says good-bye, realizing that the visit wasn't as bad as she had expected. In fact, she is feeling less agitated, even rather relaxed. After her niece leaves, the aunt notices that her heart is racing and she is feeling upset. Then her hip begins to ache and she has to call the nurse for a pain killer. She doesn't really know what happened.

What did happen? Clearly, there was an energy transfer from the niece to her aunt through the interaction of their auric fields, but the result in this case was detrimental. The niece arrived feeling irritable and somewhat resentful at having to visit her aunt. As a result, the energy that she unconsciously transferred served only to aggravate her aunt's already compromised system. It could not be used to help the older woman's body heal itself.

In another example of auric energy transfer, two friends meet for lunch. Karen is a chronic complainer and today she is also rather depressed. Lisa, on the other hand, arrives feeling quite well. During lunch, Karen talks endlessly about all the troubles she has had during the past week, and all the people who have let her down. Lisa listens sympathetically and before long, begins to feel sorry for Karen. By the time lunch is over, Lisa realizes that she is feeling tired and drained. Karen says good-bye and leaves feeling quite happy and, temporarily at least, relieved of her depression.

Let's examine what happened. Karen, through her constant complaining, was communicating a need. The ego defence was crying, "Nobody cares about me," a silent accusation which aroused Lisa's guilt and caused her to feel sorry for Karen. Lisa got caught up in her friend's self-centred neediness. She began to feel guilty that she was happy while her friend was suffering. Because she felt sorry for Karen, Lisa wished she could do something to help. As a result, she opened herself up, allowing her energy to flow over to Karen. The flow of energy can occur simply by virtue of having a surplus on one side and a shortage on the other.

What does *feeling sorry* really mean and where does it come from? As children, when we misbehaved and our parents showed disappointment or anger, we learned, often painfully, what it was to feel bad or guilty. When our parents were upset for their own reasons, we would often assume that we were somehow responsible. "I'm sorry mummy, I'm sorry," is the cry of a devastated child who is taking on the guilt for his parent's unhappiness. In the same way that some of us carry our infant trust into adulthood, we can also have difficulty as adults in breaking our childhood habit of *feeling sorry*, together with its associated feelings of guilt. Unless we break this habit, we will never learn to become aware of our own needs. After all, our first responsibility is to ourselves.

The best way to protect ourselves in situations like these is to realize that we are not responsible for the other person's state of mind. This realization keeps the door to our body psyche closed, so that our energy won't just flow out. This doesn't mean that we can't feel sad for our friends' misfortunes. We can always offer support and a listening ear. But it is important that we stay in control of our own psyches. We need to be honest about both our ability to help and our limitations. We must be aware of how much energy we can share.

It is clear that energy plays a major role in our psychological and physical well-being. Ignorance of that fact prevents us from making the most of the great variety of treatments available. Many of us tend to place too much faith in so-called 'healers,' whether doctors or others, giving them the entire responsibility for our health. We forget that they are merely facilitators to the healing mechanisms within our own bodies and that we must take back some of the responsibility for ourselves. This involves choosing facilitators with whom we feel comfortable and who acknowledge the importance of our own crucial role in the healing process. The power to control and monitor the psyche and its energies resides within ourselves and ultimately enables us to mobilize the healer within.

If we want the body to heal itself, we must work with the energies of both the mind and the body in combination. For example, if the body needs rest to replenish its energies, but the mind is worrying about paying the mortgage, the brain will burn up the body's energy reserves, and healing will be hindered. In order for physical healing to occur, the mind has to allow time for the body to be sick.

One way to protect and enhance our physical well-being is to take control of our thoughts. This might involve finding a way of controlling our anxieties, or learning to think more constructively. Becoming aware of our thoughts and their impact is one of the roots of spirituality. Using the brain in an unproductive way is like leaving the furnace going with all the windows open; it burns energy without benefit. Of all our organs, the brain is the biggest consumer of energy. Every action, response and thought uses up energy, which must be replaced by the body's fuel cell. Energy is the key to health and healing and, as such, we must use it wisely.

Questions

How can we create the best conditions for healing?

The body is like a fish swimming in a stream. If the stream is polluted, the fish will be tainted; if it is fresh, the fish will be healthy. The same is true of our body; its condition will be dependent on the quality of the energy within which it exists.

Thus, our first task in healing is to make sure that the body is in the most healthy energy environment possible. We create this environment with our own state of mind. If we are angry that the body is sick, or impatient for it to get well, we jeopardize the healing process. We must treat the body lovingly, neither ignoring its discomfort, nor forgetting that it is the psyche's vehicle.

Our physical surroundings are also important. These include the room in which we rest, the kind of lighting we use, the music we listen to, and the people we allow into our space. Just as the energy in which our body is bathed concerns us, so too does the energy we take into our body in the form of food. We must choose the foods that have the strongest healing properties and give us the most energy without overburdening our digestive system.

By far the most important ingredient in healing is time. Once, a man came to see me about his leg, which had been injured six months earlier and was still causing him pain. His job involved standing on his feet for up to four hours at a time and this was becoming more and more difficult for him. He feared that he might have to use a cane. Diagnostic imagery showed that his leg was outside the flowing aura, suggesting that he had been trying to mentally escape from his pain. The leg itself didn't show any inflammation but it was quite dark and difficult to enter psychically. It was apparent that a lot of internalized mind had accumulated in his leg, hampering the healing process.

I suggested a breathing exercise combined with visualization, called 'mind breathing,' to help him clear the energy blockage in his leg. This would take twenty minutes of his time, twice a day. He replied that he didn't have the time.

Many of us are unwilling to allow time to heal; we are impatient to get back to what we consider to be more important, whether it be a job, a relationship or recreation. If healing is our goal, then we must be prepared to make it a priority in our lives.

What does it mean to put 'mind over matter' and does it really work as a tool for healing?

Putting mind over matter is a method by which the mind systematically ignores physical reality. If someone has a pain, for example, he might think about something else in the hope that ignoring it will make it go away.

A keyboard player came to see me because he was having a problem with his left hand. About a year earlier, he had begun to feel pain in the hand from time to time. Since then, it had lost more and more flexibility until he was completely unable to use it. When I did diagnostic imagery, I could not psychically view the left hand. With my eyes open, I could see a complete person, left hand and all; with my eyes closed, I saw everything but the left hand. My first question to him was, "What did you do to your left hand?" He told me that, whenever he felt pain in his hand, he tried to ignore it, putting 'mind over matter.' Over the period of time that he was ignoring it, his hand went from bad to worse. He was now considering an operation on the carpal tunnel, based on the recommendation of his doctor. However, he was told that having the operation was no guarantee that he would be able to play keyboards again.

This man had psychically 'killed' his own hand by denying its existence. By putting 'mind over matter'—neither listening nor responding to the pain—he had, in fact, withdrawn the energies from his hand, to the extent that he could no longer feel its pain. No operation could bring back the hand's psyche. Unless the energies were allowed to return, healing would be drastically hampered.

I suggested that, instead of having an operation right away, he wait until his hand was psychically part of his body again. In order to achieve this, I had him imagine his hand to be a loved one, instructing him to hold it in his arms, stroke and nurture it. As the pain returned, he took medication for a period of time to make it more manageable. In addition, I used energy manipulation to help him psychically 're-own' his hand. Several months later, his hand had regained its flexibility and was no longer painful.

Pain is a signal our minds use to monitor the performance and condition of our bodies. It is like a barometer that measures our physical health. Ignoring the pain may make it go away temporarily, but it will never solve the underlying problem.

Why is it that you can have physical symptoms of illness, yet be told there is nothing wrong with you, or that "it's all in your mind?"

Modern medicine deals with a physical model of health which does not include the psyche. If, despite our physical symptoms, nothing is found to be wrong with the body, the doctor, often in frustration, may conclude that "it's all in your mind." The mind is, in effect, telling the body that it is sick and, as a result, we can develop real symptoms of illness without being physically ill. This can happen for a variety of reasons. One is that we may have learned that being sick brings us attention which we would not otherwise get. This is largely an unconscious process, controlled by the ego defence. Once our need is acknowledged—through getting the right kind of attention from our doctor—the 'illness' may disappear.

Often, however, the sickness is not *in* the mind, but *caused by* the mind. In these cases, too, there may be real symptoms for which no physical origin can be found. However, the body psyche is clearly malfunctioning, usually as a result of an energy disturbance brought on by internalized mind. We could call this a psychological illness that manifests itself in the body's energies. These are genuine illnesses, even though they are not normally diagnosed. Let's look at a few examples.

A professional cellist came to see me because he had lost the use of his right arm and hand, and could no longer control his bow. He was devastated because his doctor, after finding nothing physically wrong with him, told him that it was all in his mind.

When I looked at him psychically, his right shoulder and arm appeared very dark, almost black. I could not see any energy flow in or around the limb. Over the next few months, I taught him how to manipulate the energies in his arm and release them from his body. During this time, I also learned what had caused the problem to begin with. As a youngster, he had been very angry because his older brother, who excelled at school and sports, got all his parents' attention, while his own musical accomplishments were ignored. As a result, he began to feel that he was second best. He started using the cello as a way to get rid of his anger, fantasizing during his long practice sessions about showing his brother up. He carried this attitude with him into adulthood, and the arm continued to be the dumping ground for his internalization. This was a long-term psychological process by which the mind slowly crippled its own body psyche.

In another case, a woman in her mid-fifties came to see me with rapidly failing vision, reduced hearing, and an inability to concentrate. She held a responsible office position which was now in jeopardy. She had been through numerous medical tests, all of which came back negative. When I looked at her psychically, I did not see any of her flowing aura emerging from the top of her head. Searching for the auric flow, I found that it emerged from her body around the sternum and upper back. In addition, the energy was moving quite slowly. As I followed the energy flow upwards through her body, I encountered a dark, solid mass of energy extending from one shoulder to the other and up into her neck.

It was not surprising that her vision, hearing and mental faculties were failing; there was virtually no auric flow through her neck into the head.

I asked her whether she had recently been through a very stressful experience. She didn't hesitate to disclose that her husband had died not long ago, but she seemed to have come to terms with that. I remained puzzled about what could have caused the energy block, and I continued to probe into the recent events in her life. Eventually, with great reluctance, she told me that she had witnessed a terrible act within her own family. She felt she should inform the police, but could not bring herself to do so because it would mean getting a loved one into trouble. She couldn't bear to report the incident, nor could she live with the knowledge. For the past eight months, she had been struggling with the dilemma.

In that period of time, she had produced a vast amount of mind energy which could not be expelled, so instead, it was internalized. Her illness, no less real for not having a physical origin, was not *in* the mind, but *caused by* the mind. After a period of working with the energies to create a passageway through the blockage, together with some counselling, the auric flow was partially re-established through the neck and head. Her vision, hearing and concentration quickly improved.

In a third case, previously internalized mind energy moved into an injured area that had an energy deficit. Instead of contributing to the healing process, the mind energy hampered it. The man, a house painter, had lost his balance and fallen off a stool, breaking his arm just below the shoulder. Although the bone healed, he was still having problems moving his arm three months later. He was receiving physiotherapy, but the damaged muscles would not recover. When I looked at him psychically, I saw that the energy around his upper arm and shoulder was rather dark and that there was very little energy flowing into the arm.

Because of the injury, the arm and shoulder required a large amount of energy to repair themselves. Normally it would be drawn from reserves elsewhere in the body but, in this case, it was internalized mind that moved to the injured site. In order to restore the body's healing powers, energy manipulation was required to move the internalized mind away from the arm and shoulder.

Can energy manipulation be harmful?

Yes, in several ways. First, anyone who convinces us that he is a healer, rather than a facilitator, creates a potentially dangerous situation. When we believe that a person has the *power to heal* or is an instrument of a higher power (i.e. 'does God's work'), we tend to trust him unquestioningly and give him complete responsibility for our well-being. Once we have done this, we may neglect to take care of our bodies, or we may ignore medical advice, the result being that we end up in a worse condition than before the 'healing.' In addition, when someone who views himself as a 'healer' abdicates responsibility to a higher power, he may refuse to be held accountable for his actions. If his energy work has a negative effect, he may claim that he was only an instrument, or that it was 'God's will.'

Second, because the 'healer,' particularly in a religious setting, receives so much respect and even reverence, the position may be sought after by those who are in need of self-validation. These people are especially likely to view themselves as healers rather than facilitators and, because of their own feelings of inadequacy, they may behave competitively. Even when their own energies are depleted and they are in need of healing, they may be reluctant to relinquish their position as 'healer.' As a result, they will continue to practise healing work even when they are in a negative state of mind, often doing more harm than good. Such people are likely to encourage dependence or 'psychic slavery' because their own needs will always come first.

Third, because the human psyche is incredibly complex, energy manipulation can affect many different aspects of it, including the mind. For this reason, the facilitator must take it upon himself to become a student of the mind, not least of all his own. If he does not know himself—his limitations, his mental tendencies, and so on—he may inadvertently harm his patient. For example, he may not be equipped to deal with the psychological response of a needy patient who looks to him as the parent-nurturer and, as a result, becomes dependent upon him. It may even be the case that the patient has come not so much to be healed as to get attention. This type of patient seeks out a facilitator who will give him the attention he wants—most likely someone who needs to be needed, in other words, a 'caretaker.' In cases such as these, the needs of both patient and facilitator are being met, but usually at the expense of any real healing. Because the patient's 'illness' sustains the relationship, no attempt is made to treat it. When treatment is sought for an apparently physical illness that is actually caused by a needy ego, the true need may be overlooked. If this is the case, the healing, if successful at all, will be short-lived.

Fourth, the facilitator's own emotional conflicts may impact upon the patient during the energy work, especially if the facilitator is unaware of them. If, for example, he is angry or under a lot of stress, he will transfer some of that negative energy to the patient, who may then be left with feelings which he is unable to identify or deal with.

A fifth potential cause of harm arises if the facilitator does not have a good understanding of the energies he is manipulating, or of the proper way to manipulate them. He may claim that he has removed negative energies from the body when they have merely been moved around *within* the body. This may give relief in one area, but create problems elsewhere.

Whether he is simply manipulating or transferring energy, or acting as an instrument of a 'higher' power (in other words, drawing on energies outside himself), the facilitator must remain accountable for his actions and any guidance he offers. After undergoing treatment, a person may temporarily feel better and, as a result, he may neglect important medical instructions. It is essential that a facilitator advise the patient to heed any advice his doctor has given him. Although the outcome of a healing is not ultimately within the facilitator's control, that doesn't mean that he can give the responsibility for the patient's health to someone else.

As with modern medical practice, traditional methods of healing, such as energy manipulation, acupuncture, herbal medicine and rituals for psychic and spiritual purification, require many years of study to master. Yet today, many of us think we can become healers after attending a few courses or participating in a weekend workshop. This is not to say that we can't be facilitators of healing in the early stages of our training. Since time immemorial, people with little or no training have practised the 'laying on of hands,' frequently with very good results. If, however, we start believing that we are 'healers' and neglect to consider the effects of our interventions on the whole of the psyche being, then

111

we enter dangerous territory. As facilitators, we must always be accountable, even when we practise within a religious setting.

How does visualization make changes in the physical body?

When we learn to focus our minds with full concentration, it is like taking sunlight and focusing it through a magnifying glass at a small point. The temperature of the focal point becomes many times greater than that of the light itself and can be used as a tool for starting a fire. Similarly, as the mind focuses on a single point, all the energy produced by the brain is directed to that point and can be used as a tool to bring about a change. While any visualization has the potential to become a psychic reality, a focused visualization *is* a psychic reality. Because the body lives within and is controlled by the psyche, physical changes may follow.

Is it possible to release internalized mind energy?

As we explained in a previous chapter, 'secondary mind' is an accumulation of internalized energy that has built up over a long period of time. Whenever our ego systems are challenged, this energy is reactivated and becomes the driving force, or the fuel, of the ego defence. Because internalized mind is an integral part of who we are, it is very difficult, though not impossible, to release it without first becoming conscious of its origin. Even if we were to release the energy through psychic means, unless we address the problem that caused it to be internalized, it would very quickly be replaced with more of the same.

The first step in removing internalized energy is to embark on a path of personal growth with the aid of a guide, therapist or teacher. That person can help us understand who we are and why we have internalized. The learning process that leads to personal growth involves becoming aware of and peeling away the layers of the ego defence, so that the ego can be nourished. This process, sometimes called 'ego burning,' can be extremely painful. It causes us to become aware of what Carl Jung called our *shadow*: our dishonesty, manipulative behaviour, self-centredness—all the personality traits we would prefer not to know we have. At first we may be devastated, wondering how we could possibly have been wrong or bad for so many years. Eventually, however, we learn to see our past actions not as mistakes, but as the best possible choices we could have made, based on the information we had at the time. As we move towards self-acceptance and the ego defence is peeled away, the ego can begin to take in nourishment, in the form of compliments from others and acknowledgment of our own achievements.

Another way of facilitating personal growth is through a path of spiritual development, although it's important to realize that not all paths lead to personal growth. Some of the methods that can provide us with the challenge to grow are study, meditation and labour. Each path emphasizes one particular method more than others. At the same time, the teacher may challenge us personally, drawing attention to our habits of thought and behaviour. Although energy release can happen spontaneously during any of these practices, they all require close supervision and regular access to the teacher or her aides.

Release of internalized energy can also be effected by means of a therapeutic relationship in which such disciplines as bodywork, breathing or imaging techniques are used. The process of energy release can be extremely difficult. It may sometimes seem as though the ego defence is screaming in protest, not wanting to let go of the energy, which is, after all, a part of itself. This is why certain unhealthy patterns of behaviour are hard to change. Often, as the energy is released, new or unfamiliar feelings or behaviours may surface, which the therapist can help us understand.

Whatever methods of growth and energy release we choose, the process may take as much as one year for every six to ten years of life. As we work through it, we need to remember that internalized energy cannot be permanently removed unless we first allow ourselves the opportunity for growth and learning. Without them, we would continue to waste our energy by internalizing, and there would be no benefit to the soul.

How does prayer help in healing?

The body needs energy to repair itself. When a friend is ill and we pray for her, we are, in effect, asking God to intervene and heal her. We feel helpless to do anything ourselves. As we pray, we usually visualize the person and, in doing so, we direct our energy to them. If the person heals quickly, it may be that our prayers were answered. But, even by simply sending energy, we make a difference.

On the other hand, all the energy in the world can not help a person who doesn't want to get well.

How does spontaneous remission occur?

Spontaneous remission is often not very spontaneous at all! Usually, before it happens, the person will have undergone a transformation of some magnitude; they will have 'opened up' and, as a result, become able to receive nurturing, whether in the form of energy or emotional support. The energy and support can come from friends, family, therapists or doctors, and spiritual experiences may also play an important part. If the illness is related to internalized mind, once the ego system is no longer on the defensive, the energy can be released. This is true whether the release occurs through emotional catharsis, a momentary enlightenment, or some other event.

A personal transformation often involves a realization about oneself in relation to one's body; specifically, coming to know that the psyche never dies or realizing that it needs to be healed before it can look after its body. In both cases, the focus shifts from a preoccupation with the physical aspect and the accompanying fear of death to an acceptance of the psyche and of *what is*. With this awareness comes the ability to know just what kind of emotional support and environmental setting one needs to facilitate healing, and to recognize the kind of people and surroundings which will hamper it. Life-threatening illnesses are most likely to create the conditions for such a transformation.

CHAPTER 6

Spirituality:
What place in Wellness?

What is spirituality? What does it mean to lead a spiritual life? I once asked a group of people what the word *spirituality* meant to them. Their answers, though certainly significant for them, did not, in most cases, offer any insight into the pursuit of a spiritual way of life. They gave such definitions as "getting in touch with my higher self," "something to do with God the creator and the spirit," "being considerate of my neighbour," "something undefinable but very real," "an altered state of mind, when suddenly I am no longer in this world," "feeling that something beyond me is in charge," "connecting with my inner truth," and "something I feel when I'm outdoors in nature."

Many of us think of spirituality as mysterious or beyond our grasp, something inner or hidden, or something relating to a higher power. Consequently, we believe that, in order to be spiritual, we have to remove ourselves from the necessities of everyday life. But it is in those very necessities that the essence of spirituality lies. Leading a spiritual life means taking responsibility for ourselves at the most primal level. It means rooting ourselves firmly in reality and developing an understanding of who we are and how we relate to our environment. The following story illustrates this.

During the depression, there was a family with two children. Although work was hard to come by, the man found a job and came home at the end of his first day with a bag full of food. The woman divided the food into four equal portions, and they all ate. She upheld the doctrine of 'share and share alike,' believing that if she did the 'right thing,' the family would be looked after. The next day, the following day, and the day after, she divided the food in the same way. This continued for seven days, but then, on the eighth day, the man came home with his bag of food only half full. He hadn't had enough energy to work the whole day. The day after that, he was sick and could not work at all. Soon after, the entire family perished.

In another village, there was another family, also with two children. The man also brought home a bag full of food each day. The woman took half of the food and divided it into three portions, with which she fed herself and her children. The other half she gave to her husband. The next day, the following day, and the day after, she did the same thing. Much later, when the depression ended, the family had survived.

The woman in the first family did not take responsibility for her family's survival, but instead gave the responsibility to a 'higher' power. She blindly followed a dogma that she had learned as a child and never really questioned. It didn't occur to her to consider its practical outcome. In contrast, the woman in the second family went against the popular teaching of 'share and share alike,' realizing that, in this situation, its application would have disastrous consequences. Her decision was a selfish one; she knew that if her husband was well nourished he could continue to provide for her and their children. Her desire to ensure her family's survival, even if it meant rejecting a traditional moral value, is a true sign of spirituality.

The idea that an understanding of spirituality begins at a primal level, and not an elevated or 'higher' level, can be illustrated in another way. Consider a forest. If we look at it from above the trees, we can only see the foliage. To really see the forest, however, we have to stand among the trees, not above them. From this vantage point, we can see the roots, the trunks, and the limbs of the trees. We can feel the moist soil and watch the wildlife and the insects, all of which help to maintain the life of the trees. It is the magnificent foliage that gathers sunlight in order to give us oxygen, but without the intricate system of branches, trunks and roots, the foliage could not exist. In fact, the entire forest started out with a single seed that, in all likelihood, was carried there by the wind or in the droppings of an animal.

In the same way that the forest is more than just a canopy of leaves, spirituality is more than just the contemplation of thoughts and ideas. By themselves, these thoughts are of little use. Spirituality begins with the acknowledgment that we are carriers of the seed and that our sexuality is integral to our being. This is not to say that thought is outside the realm of spirituality. On the contrary, it is the essence of spirituality. It's not so much the object of our thoughts as the way in which we think that reflects our spirituality, however. The following story illustrates this point.

A family with two children lived in a country where the winters were very cold. The woman's old winter coat was almost threadbare; it would not serve her for another winter. The family decided to save some household money every week so that she could buy a new coat.

One day, her husband noticed that the local department store was having a sale on winter coats for $95. After counting up all the money they had saved, they were delighted to find that they had 97 dollars and some change.

The following morning, the woman got up early and took the bus to the store. She found the coat rack with the sign saying, "Special: $95." At the end of the rack was a coat in her size and the perfect shade of rust for her complexion. She put it on and stood in front of the three-way mirror, admiring how well it looked on her. "This will surely keep me warm," she thought.

In the mirror she noticed another coat rack with a sign that read: "Sale: $175." As she walked towards it, she saw a beautiful tan-coloured coat with a large imitation fur collar. She put it on, admiring herself in the mirror for a very long time. Her glance kept coming to rest on the price tag, as though she were hoping that the price would magically change. A sales lady approached her and said, "My, that coat does flatter you, and it is such an unbeatable price!" "Thank you," the woman replied, "but I'm only looking." Reluctantly, she took it off and went back to the first rack to get the less expensive one.

The children ran home from school that day. Before they even took off their own boots and coats, they asked excitedly, "Mom, did you get your coat?" Their mother replied, "Of course I did. Now take off your boots and sit down at the table." But the children insisted on seeing the new coat first. Although she wasn't very eager to oblige them, she put it on for them to see. The children thought she looked very beautiful. They stroked the fabric and admired the buttons. Their mother said, "You should have seen the other one. It had a fur collar and bigger pockets."

When her husband came home from work, he too was eager to see the new coat. She didn't really want to show it to him; it was just a coat, after all. Her husband persisted and, reluctantly, she went to put it on. Her husband said, "How beautiful you look. I worked overtime and have some extra money. Let's go out and have dinner so I can show you off in your new coat." His wife replied, "But you should have seen the other one with the fur collar."

There will always be people who go through life wishing and wanting, unwilling to accept the reality of their lives—in effect, choosing to be unhappy. The woman in the story made a decision to be unhappy for as long as she owns her coat. Each time she puts it on, she'll be thinking about the other one—the one she couldn't afford—and how much more luxurious it was. Because of her choice to be unhappy, she denied both herself and her family the joy of celebrating her purchase. She prevented her husband and children, who struggled to put money aside throughout the year, from enjoying the fruits of their efforts. Worst of all, her self-centredness made them feel that they failed to make her happy, and as a result, an opportunity to nurture the children's developing egos was lost.

One of the roots of spirituality is the acceptance of *what is,* which means choosing not to be unhappy. When we fail to accept reality, always wishing for something we don't have, we live in a state of illusion or fantasy, believing that what will make us happy lies just around the corner. As a result, we place no value on the things we do have, or the labour that enabled us to obtain those things. Without that sense of value, we have no foundation upon which to build a spiritual life.

Another aspect of spirituality is an awareness of the psyche's relationship to physical health. This involves becoming conscious of our thinking processes and taking responsibility for our ego system, both the 'I am' and the 'I am not.' It means not blaming our problems on those who shaped us or using their shortcomings as an excuse for our behaviour. It does not necessarily mean being in a loving state of mind all the time, but it does mean becoming honest with ourselves.

Spirituality is also about taking responsibility for the energies that we send out both through our thoughts and our auras, realizing that our state of mind, whether loving or angry, has an impact on those near us.

Recall the woman who visited her aunt in the hospital and ended up upsetting her aunt's energies.

Because she had no knowledge of the psyche, she could neither take responsibility for, nor be honest about, her negative attitude and its likely impact. The woman's motivation for visiting her aunt was not to give pleasure but, rather, to fulfill an obligation; she felt she *should* go. As a result, the energy that she passed on to her aunt had a harmful effect rather than a healing one. She may have even believed that visiting her aunt was a spiritual act. But spirituality is not about doing things for others in order to satisfy our own 'shoulds.' Such an act can only be spiritual if it arises from true kindness.

For most of us, the sense of obligation—getting caught up in the 'shoulds'—is usually derived from guilt. Along with such other negative and unproductive thought patterns as worrying, harbouring anger, rehashing old scenarios, or otherwise 'spinning our wheels,' guilt prevents us from evaluating our feelings and actions honestly. Because the 'I am not' is constantly seeking nourishment or validation, it often makes us do things for the wrong reasons. We are often angry with ourselves when we do these things, yet we don't know why we do them. Being spiritual does not necessarily mean saying "no" to everyone who tries to take advantage of us, but it does mean that we have the choice to decide how much energy or time we want to devote to others. It is not spiritual to deny our own needs and invest our energies in those who are never satisfied and give us nothing in return.

The farmer will tend to his orchard with great care as long as his trees can bear fruit. A woman will tend to her plants as long as they can bring forth flowers. Both nurture what will grow and what will give them something in return. The farmer would not tend to a dead tree, nor would the woman water a stick. But how often have we watered a stick, knowing that it will not flower and that our energies are being wasted? Because we think that spirituality has to do with putting other's needs before our own, we are afraid to say "no" to being taken for granted, manipulated or otherwise misused.

Many of us have difficulty saying "no." We not only fear the other person's reaction—they might be hurt and upset, or angry with us—we also want to protect ourselves from the guilt and remorse that accompany the belief that we have done something wrong. Therefore, we often decide to say "yes" to avoid creating bad feelings. But if this is our choice, then we shouldn't complain about the way we are being treated. The fact is, there will be a price to pay whether we say "yes" or "no," but when we choose to say "yes," we may never stop paying.

Many of us have been brought up to view selfishness as a negative trait. We are taught that putting our needs before others' and saying "no" to them is selfish and, therefore, bad. This viewpoint is instilled in us from childhood and, as a result, it is very difficult to change. If, as children, we were made to feel badly when we put out own needs first, we may become 'yoked,' or negatively attached to our parents because of our need for their approval and love. That yoke is guilt and, strange as it may seem, it keeps both parties in balance until one recognizes its cost.

Once we realize that our compliance has made us neglect our own well-being, we can start to unlearn the conditioning that causes us to feel guilty whenever we put our own needs first. But first we need to make a decision whether or not to continue along the same road. If we decide to challenge our conditioning and say "no," we need to be aware that the other person may not be ready for a similar challenge. He may go to any length to keep the yoke in place so that we will continue to fill his needs. If we feel ourselves succumbing to his attempt to make us feel guilty, we must remind ourselves that we've done nothing wrong.

Getting free of a yoke takes great courage and may be one of the hardest things we ever do. It forces us to learn to live independently, without being attached to another person by the strong ties of guilt. The person to whom we are negatively attached may be thrown off balance if we break free and, in desperation, may threaten us with anger or the withdrawal of his affection. This not only intensifies our guilt, it also makes us fearful. We may then decide that the price is too high, and relent.

If we do decide to take the risk of saying "no," and persist in the struggle until we are free, the other person may also benefit from the release. In time, he may come to realize that, in depending upon us, he has neglected to develop his own capabilities and potential for growth.

Spirituality is not having to hit a fly just because it is there. It is being aware of each action we take and knowing its reason or purpose. How often do we arrive at our destination without knowing how we got there? We spend much of our lives putting our bodies in an automatic mode while our minds are somewhere else. Not until we collide with a tree do we realize it was there. If, on the other hand, we pay attention to what we are doing, we enhance our enjoyment of it. As we walk, we can enjoy the movement of our legs and feet, while at the same time we can be aware of the trees, the houses and the people we meet along the way.

How many people enjoy peeling a potato? Most of us probably let our minds wander off somewhere else while we're doing it. Perhaps it's because we consider peeling a potato to be a menial task, unworthy of our attention. But doesn't this demonstrate that we view the nourishing of our body as an unimportant part of life? Living spiritually means deciding that, when something needs to be done, we will like doing it.

Spirituality means being aware of ourselves, our environment, and our place in the world. It means understanding our interconnectedness with nature. Spirituality means taking responsibility for the way we use—or misuse—the world's resources and the way our children will live and function in tomorrow's world. It means building ego and character, both our own and our children's, and taking responsibility for the preservation and betterment of life.

Too often we strive for spiritual development before we have attained awareness of the psyche. We want to gaze into the clouds above the treetops, but we're afraid to look at the shadows beneath the leaves. There are teachings that warn against seeking out darkness, suggesting that those who show interest in what is hidden are, at best, misguided or, at worst, evil. But for many of us, these teachings have not been able to answer some of our deepest questions. As a result, we have turned to ancient yet timeless ways, in which the psyche is an integral part of life. As we learn from these teachings, we begin to understand that the answers to our questions are not to be found in the clouds above the trees, but inside the forest, among the trees. It is here that we walk a path and become aware of the life and purpose of the forest without losing sight of the seed. In order to grow spiritually, we need to become aware of *our* purpose—to create thought—without losing sight of our physical roots. This is the path of the psyche.

Questions

What is spiritual growth?

Spiritual growth is first and foremost ego growth. As long as we are still at the stage of learning about our own ego systems, it would be premature to try and go beyond. Some people believe that, in order to achieve spiritual growth, they have to take care of their souls. But it is because of soul that we are here; the soul existed long before we were even thought of. Therefore, the soul is well able to look after itself! Even in the pursuit of spirituality, our responsibility lies only with the ego system, both the 'I am' and the 'I am not,' which is the essence of our identities. Spiritual growth has less to do with delving into the soul, immersing oneself in meditation or having out-of-body experiences than it does with learning about ourselves and 'growing up.' As soon as we begin to strive for ego growth, spiritual growth will follow.

What part do prayer and meditation play in spiritual growth?

There are a variety of ways in which prayer and meditation can play a part in our spiritual growth. First of all, they can help us recognize our place in the universe, allowing us to become part of a whole, rather than remaining separate and, there-fore, isolated. They can also help us realize our purpose if, through them, we become aware that we are in service of something greater. Other pursuits facilitated by prayer and meditation include looking within ourselves to uncover our own truths, contemplating a question about life, or reflecting upon an awareness. We can also use them as disciplines to control our thoughts and our energies so that we might become totally present in the moment. Finally, they can provide a means of getting in touch with those who may be able to teach us. [*]

Prayer and meditation, in themselves, are not enough to achieve spiritual growth, however. Labour is ultimately more relevant to spirituality, as the following story illustrates.

There was a remote village where the people had no work and could barely feed themselves. One day, when the villagers were near perishing, a stranger arrived and built a large pottery factory. Soon after, the village began to prosper. The people of the village felt indebted to him, so every morning when they arrived at the factory, they would pray to him for half an hour to express their gratitude. Again every evening, they would pray for half an hour before going home. Thus, instead of working eight hours every day, they worked only seven. One day, the man gathered all his workers together. He

---

[*] See Willemsen (forthcoming)

told them that, instead of praying, a better way to show their gratitude would be to spend the full eight hours making pottery so that the factory might be profitable, and they could all continue to prosper.

If we bring the right understanding to our labour, then it can actually become a form of meditation or prayer. If a nurse, in caring for her patients, makes all of her actions purposeful, sees her work as a service to humanity, and carries out her responsibilities with acceptance and joy, she will grow spiritually without sitting for prayer or meditation. If a person works in the service of humankind, their labour *is* the prayer.

Is happiness the goal of life?

We expend a lot of energy looking for happiness, some of us to the point of exhaustion. But is it really happiness that we are seeking, or merely an escape from our pain and emptiness? Sometimes, our search comes from a place of inner need—the 'I am not' or the unnurtured part of the ego system. But if the purpose behind our quest for happiness is really to escape from where we are, we will never discover—let alone fill—our inner need. We are like the dog running away from his own burning tail. We want to escape from our present reality but many of us are unwilling to work for a better one. I have never seen a lazy person who was happy, though I've seen hard-working people with smiles on their faces.

Unhappy people are constantly seeking nourishment for their egos yet, regardless of what they achieve, they are never satisfied. For these people, happiness is an illusory goal, like the proverbial pot of gold at the end of the rainbow. It will always escape them. On the other hand, happiness may well come to the person who practises the art of not being unhappy. Therefore, *not being unhappy* should be our goal. It is achievable; happiness is not.

If we are in a state of acceptance of 'what is,' does that mean we cannot try to change things?

Many people misunderstand what it means to be in a state of acceptance. They think it means agreeing with or submitting to whatever happens to be their lot. If this were the case, however, there would be no growth, either personal or social. Old practices would not be challenged to make way for new ones, injustices would not be righted, and personal obstacles would not be overcome.

To be in a state of acceptance means, first of all, coming to terms with those things we cannot change. For example, the temperature in Winnipeg can drop to minus 40 degrees centigrade in the winter. Those of us who live here complain about it, wish it were otherwise and dream of living elsewhere, but the reality is that we are here. We have the choice of coming to terms with the winter climate, or spending six months out of every year cursing it.

Being in a state of acceptance means seeing nature as an essential part of life, rather than an inconvenience. We often complain about rain, blaming it for spoiling our outings or ruining our clothes. However, without rain, we wouldn't have water flowing out of our taps, bread on our table, vegetables to eat, or oxygen to breathe.

We are in a state of acceptance when we acknowledge the facts of a situation, including the way we feel about it. Too often, when we can't come to terms with something we have witnessed or experienced, such as an act of abuse or a personal injustice, we explain it away, ignore it or pretend it never happened.

Acceptance also includes the recognition of who we are—the sum total of what we were taught and what we were not taught, as well as all the experiences we have had. Changes can never be made from a state of wishing we were otherwise, or by dreaming our time away in an escape from our present circumstances. Only from a foundation of acceptance can we make a thoughtful evaluation of what steps we can take to bring about change. When we do not accept ourselves, we are often too preoccupied with what is missing or hasn't been accomplished to take these steps. Perhaps we are afraid that acceptance of ourselves means submitting to our failures. But it is only through recognizing our mistakes that we learn to make changes. Once we are in complete acceptance of our total self, without excuses or regrets, we have a foundation upon which to build. We may even find that most of the building has already been completed and that we merely need to make some slight alterations.

Acceptance is not easy to achieve. Few of us have been trained to view life in a logical way or to see ourselves as an integral part of it. Instead, we cling to our illusions of how life *should* be and see ourselves as somehow separate from it. Rather than responding to and growing with the inevitable changes that take place around us, we react against them.

The spiritual masters live in a state of acceptance, but it may have taken them 20 years of practising spiritual disciplines daily to achieve it. Most people in our society will never reach that point. On the other hand, working towards acceptance is part of growth, and it is okay if we falter and make mistakes along the way. We will know that we have taken the first step when we catch ourselves complaining about something and smile as we say to ourselves, "I caught you!"

When a person is born with a handicap or, for other reasons, endures great suffering in her life, it is sometimes said, "That's her karma." What is meant by this?

First of all, what is karma? The idea of karma originates in Buddhism and is based on the belief that each person has a succession of lives. The word *karma* (from the Sanskrit: 'action or fate'), refers to the sum of a person's actions in one life which will determine his fate in the next one. Sometimes, instead of saying, "It's her karma," people will say, "It's her learning," meaning that what she has to learn or experience in this life is the result of what she failed to learn in her previous ones.

If we accept that we belong to the soul, rather than the reverse, it follows that the same is true of any of the soul's previous incarnations. Each incarnation is a separate cycle, beginning with birth. Each soul drive has its own characteristics based upon what it has obtained in previous cycles, and those characteristics take us in a particular direction. But this does not mean that we inherit a karma from a previous cycle. While we do accumulate karma during the physical (i.e. embodied) part of our life cycle, it is never carried over from one cycle to another.*

Sometimes we have difficulty accepting all the misfortunes that seem to come our way. We have trouble comprehending why some of us are born

* See Willemsen, forthcoming

135

with handicaps and others endure great suffering. On the other hand, we may also have difficulty in dealing with the bad things that happen to us because of our own carelessness. When our lives are troubled, or we are dealt a blow, we want to know that our suffering has purpose—that it's not for nothing. People sometimes say, "It's my karma" as a way of helping themselves come to terms with their problems. This gives the same reassurance as saying "It's God's will."

Of 100 trees that a farmer plants, 97 will grow straight and tall; three will be crooked. The same is true in the animal world: there will be runts in some litters. It is impossible for every part of the natural world to be without flaw or blemish. Because humans are such complex life forms, we are especially subject to imperfection. We are composed of a body, a psyche and an ego system, each of which is complex in itself. Most of us will have or acquire some sort of handicap in at least one aspect of our being.

Life is full of opportunities for growth and learning. Those of us with handicaps may have the greatest opportunity of all. This is not to say that there is virtue in suffering or that it is our purpose or karma to suffer. But life will surely bring suffering to most of us and, to those who succeed in overcoming it, growth.

Many people talk about the past lives of their soul. Can knowing about them help us in our life?

As we discussed earlier, we don't *have* a soul, the soul has us. Neither the soul nor its previous lives belongs to us. The characteristics of the soul and its drive, astrological influences and the shaping of our egos are all we have to work with in this life.

Because some people are dissatisfied with their lives, they decide to look to the soul for answers. They hope that the information that the soul gives up will help to explain their difficulties. They do this without first having explored their own ego systems. If they did, they might find that the answers to their difficulties can often be found a lot closer to home than in the soul's previous lives.

Spiritual growth depends on what we do with our ego systems. By focusing on the past lives of the soul, we avoid taking responsibility for ourselves. The trials of some other identity become our excuse for the way we feel and behave. There is little difference between saying, "I feel this way because my mother never held me" and saying, "I feel this way because I was abandoned in a past life."

Sometimes, after reliving a traumatic experience during 'past life regression' work, a person will say that he has come to understand where his difficulties began and he can now deal with them. But just because the experience was transformative, it does not necessarily follow that he has relived one

137

of *his* past lives. When someone experiences something very deeply, as is often the case in hypnotic regression, it often has a profound effect upon him. However, this would be the case whether he was fed information through suggestion, recalled a previously unconscious memory of his own, or relived an actual experience from another identity's life.

In the pursuit of knowledge about humanity and the universe, there may be some value to exploring this territory. Not knowing how deeply affected you may be by a regression experience, however, you must exercise caution. How well do you know your own ego system? Are you prepared for the psychological impact of the knowledge you may obtain? How much experience does your facilitator have? Is she equipped to deal with your possible disorientation and to help you integrate the experience? What are her spiritual beliefs? How might her views influence you in a moment of vulnerability?

There's no question that the soul has had other cycles before our own. Sometimes, under certain circumstances, it will surrender memories from those cycles. This can even happen spontaneously. Before we decide to pursue this information, however, we need to be fully aware of our purpose in doing so.

In some teachings it is said that our egos stand in the way of truth, and that we need to set the ego aside if we want to truly know ourselves. What is meant by that?

To my way of thinking, we have too little understanding of ourselves and our purpose to recognize, let alone understand, what truth is. The basis for a person's truth is what he was taught and what he believes as a result, not *what is*.

If we wish to embark upon the pursuit of truth, we need to accept ourselves completely as we are now, realizing that, just as the universe is in constant motion, we too are constantly changing. Our truth, therefore, is also changing.

Without the ego there is no truth or learning. Therefore, it can never stand in the way of truth. Nor can we set the ego defence aside, as it is just as much a part of us as the ego. It is the ego defence which hides from, or ignores truth. Before we can search for truth, we have to become honest about ourselves. Once the 'I am' becomes secure and we experience ourselves as part of a whole rather than as a separate identity, we may come to know our truth, and the ego will grow as a result.

Is there ever a time when one is ready to die?

Some people have a great fear of dying. Usually, these are people who never questioned what life was about or what their purpose was. They think that the body is all that they are and, therefore, they fear the pain signals that tell them there is something wrong with it. Instead of seeing death as an integral part of the life cycle, they see it as an ending. Such people are never ready to die.

Dissatisfaction or anger with our lives may also make us feel unprepared, even when it is our time to die. If we feel that there is something incomplete or unfinished, we may have difficulty letting go. Our own families may even hold us back from dying, making us feel that we are abandoning them.

If, on the other hand, we feel that our life has had purpose, if we have made a contribution and received our reward, if we can look back and feel good, but our body is now struggling to support us, then we may be ready to die. For those of us who are ready for it, dying can be a joyful experience.

What does it mean to walk a path?

Walking a path is a way of discovering and developing one's self and one's spirituality. Specifically, it helps us become aware of our relationship to everything around us. In our journey of self-discovery, we are guided by a teacher who is often, herself, a student of the path. Walking a path involves learning what it means to be of service and being willing to labour in the pursuit of growth and learning. This pursuit is not a self-centred one; it is never undertaken for the sake of personal gain.

There is not a big difference between being spiritual and taking the first steps along a path. As we've seen, spirituality involves acting consciously and taking responsibility for our behaviour and our thoughts, as well as our relations with others. Both entail an awareness of the way in which we lead our lives. Both can be taught, although the lessons of spirituality are frequently passed on by a parent or through the teachings of a religion. Some people ask if it is possible to walk a path without a teacher. This is like asking whether we can sail the ocean without a compass. Some people say they can.

While there are many different paths of spiritual growth, they all have one thing in common, and that is following a discipline. Some paths are based upon a religion and involve worship or prayer. Others may teach through such disciplines as meditative exercises, chanting, physical movements or postures. Still others use labour or some other service as a vehicle for learning. Many paths combine all of these elements.

There are some paths, however, that lead not to growth and awareness, but to disappointment and intolerance. These are the ones that make promises or require us to accept a dogma without question.

Sometimes the path we choose to walk is less important than the way in which we walk it. Is it something we do every waking moment, or just one or two hours a week? Do we make a commitment to follow one particular path for a period of time, or do we shift from one to another, always feeling dissatisfied? Do we bring something to the path we walk, or do we only expect things from it?

As we follow the path, we should always be questioning, or else our minds will not be open and receptive. Learning can happen at any moment along the way. When we walk a path, we should walk *with* the teacher, not *behind* her. This way, rather than merely following in her footsteps, we will be making our own. If we expect to be taught or lectured to, we are not walking a path but following a doctrine. How far we walk will depend upon our eagerness—but not our impatience—to experience and learn for ourselves.

Many people ask about the goals of a path. But if we walk a path with a particular goal in mind—spiritual enlightenment, for example, or knowledge—we will be walking for the wrong reason. We should not so much seek to acquire knowledge, as to *become*. If we adopt tunnel vision, we miss out on the opportunity to make discoveries along the way. We keep our psyches closed, in effect.

Although reaching a specific end point should not be our purpose in walking a path, it's important that we make some forward progress. Some people have followed spiritual disciplines for many years but have never actually completed one full step along a path. Imagine the different paths as spokes on a wheel, each one leading from the hub to the rim. Some people want to explore many of the spokes but spend only enough time to get a sample of each. They dilly-dally around the hub, accumulating a lot of superficial knowledge about each spiritual discipline, but never seriously embark on any one path.

Do we have to follow one path all of our lives?

There is a story about two teachers from different parts of the country who were travelling with some of their students. One day, they met at an inn and greeted each other joyfully. As they sat drinking tea and sharing stories, they heard a commotion. Outside, they found their students noisily arguing about which path was the better one.

Each path has its own way of teaching and its own way of revealing things. No one is *better* than any other; each brings about a different kind of learning. Although two paths travel in different directions, they ultimately take us to the same place. All the spokes of the wheel lead to the same rim. When we reach that rim, having completed one part of the journey, we may experience a moment of enlightenment, after which we realize that we are merely inside another hub. At that point, we may decide to explore another path.

Is there such a thing as a bad or dangerous path?

There are some paths that are inherently bad or dangerous. But even a good path can be dangerous if we do not follow it wisely. If we fail to take responsibility for ourselves, accepting a set of beliefs without question, we put ourselves at risk. Danger also lurks when we rely on the path to become our nurturer in order to bolster a fragile ego.

Many young people join the military service because their lives do not provide them with the support or the boundaries they need. The service gives them a purpose and a sense of belonging and becomes, in effect, the supportive parent. As soldiers, they know what is expected of them and feel protected. The security and discipline that the military provides serves to alleviate their feelings of confusion and anxiety.

Sometimes, we follow a spiritual path for similar reasons, looking to it for security or support. This can be dangerous if we are dealing with deep emotional needs, unless we seek additional help, such as psychotherapy. Not until we come to terms with our emotional needs can we set the ego defence aside. If our path is blocked by ego defence, we close ourselves off from the growth and learning that a path can bring and we risk adding disappointment or a sense of failure to an already troubled mind.

As we mentioned, there are some paths that are harmful in and of themselves. These are paths that promote a rigid doctrine, demand absolute loyalty, and forbid questions. Those of us with damaged ego systems are particularly vulnerable. We are led to believe that the path offers salvation and will take care of us into eternity. When it fails to provide for our needs, the disappointment may have serious psychological consequences. This is a high price to pay for the illusion of well-being.

The path we choose need not interfere with our religious beliefs, although it may alter them at some point. Difficulty can arise when a path from one culture or religion is brought into a different one, without taking the values and beliefs of the latter into consideration. Such a path may be more than simply a way of learning; it may also carry with it the values and practices of the culture in which it originates. In order to follow such a path, the student will have to adopt many of that culture's values. Not only are these values extraneous to walking a path, they can also cause us to abandon those of our own culture, which probably serve us better.

Paths that have been imported from other cultures often become popular with younger people, as an alternative to their own religious teachings which may have let them down. These people tend to treat the path as a religion or a form of worship, rather than a way of learning, accepting without question the beliefs that accompany it. Again, the fault here lies not so much in the path itself, as in the way it is followed.

145

Do we have to follow a path in order to lead a spiritual life?

Many of us have been taught spiritual values, but frequently fail to apply them. We go to church and park our car in a space reserved for the disabled, or we pray on Sunday and curse our neighbour on Monday.

For some people, the path through life is naturally one of teaching, sharing and building, like the plumber who enjoys his craft. He takes great satisfaction in handling each piece of pipe, welding or threading each fitting in place, and positioning each valve where it is required. He is glad to be a builder and of service. If he also shares his children's joys and disappointments, nurturing and building their egos, he is truly leading a spiritual life.

How important is it to have purpose in one's life?

As an integral part of life on this planet, we all have an innate need to fulfill a purpose. Just as the bee looks for honey, builds a hive, and protects the life of his queen, all for the purpose of pollinating flowers, so do we pursue physical life in order to create mind.

In the first half of our lives, we usually carry out our purpose naturally, rarely feeling the need to question it. A little girl might fulfill her purpose by playing with her dolls or looking after her pet, as practice for being a mother. A young woman fulfills her purpose when she studies for a career, looks for a mate, raises a family, and helps to build a better society for her children.

As people grow older and find themselves alone or with time on their hands, they are more likely to question their purpose. Some of them, fearing the loss of purpose, may cling to their children, instead of trying to make themselves useful elsewhere. Others may move on to new pursuits and interests, enjoying their new-found freedom. Still others may begin to wonder if there is more to life, and in doing so, they become seekers. A seeker will ask himself, possibly for the first time in his life, "What is the reason for it all?" It is very natural to reach this point in one's later years.

As we seek to understand our purpose within the greater scheme of things, our search will sometimes lead us on a spiritual path. Many paths, including those from within our own mystical traditions are, in fact, intended for the later part of our lives, as a way of preparing for the hereafter. For most of us, it is only during this period that we have the time to concentrate on spiritual disciplines or the financial means to travel large distances in pursuit of these interests.

Times are changing, however. Today, many younger people are looking to spiritual teachings in their search for purpose and identity. While the priority for most young adults is to raise children, pursue a career, or both, there is no reason why these teachings cannot play a role during this phase. Spiritual teachings can be useful, for example, in helping children to understand the world around them, as well as in helping the parents understand the purpose they fulfill by virtue of being *of service*.

Is there such a thing as perfection?

The universe is eternal; it has neither beginning nor end. It exists through generating its own life. Everything within it is in a process of continuous growth and, therefore, in a *state of perfection*.

We tend to think of perfection as an end point or a goal to be attained. From this point of view, it follows that there can be no further growth after that goal is reached. A flower in full bloom is only a moment away from decay. Thus, our goal should not be to *attain* perfection but instead, to live in a state of perfection; in other words, to keep growing and developing.

Someone gave me a feather and said, "Isn't this perfect!" As part of the bird, it was growing and served a purpose; it was in a state of perfection. Separated from the bird, it begins to deteriorate.

As human beings, we have the power to determine whether the earth continues to be in a state of perfection or on a path towards destruction. This choice presents us with a challenge for individual growth. As we take up this challenge, we are ourselves in a state of perfection. On another level, we are in a state of perfection as long as we take responsibility for thoughts, nurture our children in order to prepare them for life, or try to understand our place in the universe.

Index of Questions

Anger
- If anger has such a negative effect on our bodies and our environment, why is it sometimes desirable to be angry? *57*

Auric field
See Energy Egg

Clairvoyance
See Psychic Readings

Death and dying
- Is there ever a time when one is ready to die? *139*

Dreams
- Can people communicate through dreams? *85*

Ego
- Can our inner child ever grow up completely? *35*
- How can we nurture our own egos? *31*
- If our 18-year old ego were fully developed, what would we be like? *37*

See also Love

See also Spiritual growth

Energy egg

- Can we become aware of our own energy or auric fields? *85*
- Is the body always in the middle of the energy egg? *62*

Energy field

See Energy Egg

Energy manipulation

See Healing

Flowing aura

- Does the soul ever stop driving the auric flow entirely? *62*
- Is it possible to learn to see or feel the flowing aura and other energies of the psyche? *86*

Healing

- Can energy manipulation be harmful? *108*
- How can we create the best conditions for healing? *101*
- How does prayer help in healing? *115*
- How does spontaneous remission occur? *115*
- How does visualization make changes in the physical body? *112*
- Is it possible to release internalized mind energy? *112*
- What does it mean to put 'mind over matter' and does it really work as a tool for healing? *101*

Healing, cont.

- Why is it that you can have physical symptoms of illness, yet be told there is nothing wrong with you, or "It's all in your mind?" *104*

Inner child

See Ego

Internalization

- Do we start to internalize in childhood? *58*

See also Healing

Karma

- When a person is born with a handicap, or for other reasons endures great suffering in her life, it is sometimes said, "That's her karma." What is meant by this? *134*

Love

- How important is love to the developing ego? *33*

See also Health

Meditation

See Spiritual growth

Mental discipline

- If we try to take control of our thoughts, do we end up losing the ability to be spontaneous, and do we close ourselves off from the psyche? *61*